Growing Up Weird:

Confessions of a Closet Medium

By Karen Crumley

Copyright©2011- Karen Crumley
All rights reserved
Purple Sage Publishing, 2011

ISBN: 9780983669012

DEDICATION
I dedicate this book to My Lord Jesus Christ, without whom I would be nothing.

ABOUT THE COVER
The scene in the picture is Terabithia, a special place on the ranch that is discussed in the book.

ACKNOWLEDGEMENTS

Many thanks go to all my family and friends, especially those who have lived through this with me and still love me. A special thanks goes to Wendy Pausewang for her technical advice and friendship. Thank you, P.B.Smith, for your editing and advice!

1 Corinthians 13:12
For now we see through a glass, darkly; but then face to face: now I know in part; but then shall I know even as also I am known.

BEGINNINGS

    I do not know exactly what woke me up. Maybe the swirling sounds forced me to open my eyes and notice the light. The intense light enveloped me, but emanated from the foot of my bed. I rubbed my eyes in an attempt to clarify what I was seeing. The brightness almost blinded me, but I could make out something in the middle. As my eyes became accustomed to the light, the view caused me to catch my breath in awe. She stood there, wrapped in radiance, speaking to me in silvery tones. Her long, beautiful hair and long white robes flowed in some invisible breeze as her musical voice delivered a mystical message. To this day, I am not able to recall exactly what she said. I only remember feeling blessed in her presence. I stared with my mouth agape in wonder, watching her mouth as it formed each word. Then, as suddenly as she had appeared, she faded completely into the darkness of my little room.
    I flung the blanket off me and hit the floor running toward the door. Throwing the door wide and running through it, I ran to my mother to tell her

what I had just seen. I could not get the words out fast enough, it seemed.

"Mommy! Did you see her?"

"Who?"

"She was there by my bed! She was all white and shiny! And she said something to me!"

My mother turned and bent down to me to give me a hug and then she told me to calm down and tell her again. I did not want to try to describe it again.

"The lady from the quarter was in my room! And she was talking to me!" The image of Lady Liberty on the old quarters was as close as I could get to a great description.

She smiled at me and said, "That's nice sweetheart."

Even at that young age, I could tell that she just did not get it.

That was the beginning. It was the first episode in an incredible lifetime of weirdness. I know now that the angel had appeared to me at the moment of my grandfather's death...and my grandfather was gifted. I believe the angel that appeared to me gave me his gifts. There are references to this kind of transfer in the Old Testament in the Second Book of Kings, Chapter two, Verses 1–14. Here, the gifts of Elijah were given to Elisha when God took Elijah up to Heaven in a chariot. I can only hope to use my grandfather's gifts as well as he did in the service of God.

You see, my grandfather died....twice. The first time he died, he had the typical near-death experience. When he returned back to his body, he reported that he followed an intense light and came to a place where he saw all of his departed loved ones across a line. Each time he tried to step across the line, they pushed him back. He kept trying, but never got to go across. He actually got angry that they would not let him come over. Finally, a big voice told him that he could not go there yet because he was not finished with his work on Earth. The next thing he knew, he woke up...thirty minutes after a doctor declared him to be dead.

He spent the next four years hoping that he could get there again soon. He knew his destination and he was looking forward to getting there just like he was going on some long-planned vacation. He wrote hymns to God and ministered to everyone on his rural mail route. He spent time with his family. When they found him in his fishing boat after he had died the second time, he had the most satisfied smile on his face. We knew he had gotten to cross the line this time. I was only four years old at the time.

BAPTIZED

	After many years, I have come to understand why the weird things began happening to me when they did. I joined a church when I turned thirteen. After a few weeks of classes, I accepted the gift of Jesus and was baptized in the Blood of Jesus Christ. I never had a clue about what would happen next since the gifts of the Spirit were not mentioned much in the teachings of my church. Now, as an adult, I am aware that when I was baptized, several gifts were activated in me by the Holy Spirit. It was as if He just switched me on like a lamp. Within a few weeks, the first episode began.
	Knock, knock. I rose up and searched in the dark toward the odd sound that woke me just as I was falling to sleep. My cat that had been peacefully sleeping at the foot of my bed suddenly rose, arched her back with her fur standing straight up and hissed at my closet. I stared into the dark, but there was nobody near the closet knocking on the wall. So, I hesitatingly closed my eyes again. A few seconds later an identical knock-knock sound came from the wall, only a few inches closer to me this time. My cat

quickly jumped off the bed and darted under it. My bed rested up against the wall at the opposite side of the room from my closet. Rubbing my eyes, I rolled over and lay there listening in the dark. Knock, knock. The sound came from the wall, again a few inches closer to me.

Now, curiosity led me to sit up and stare at the wall through the darkness. Sure enough, another two knocks fell right into the pattern, moving closer to me each time by a few inches. A chill ran up my spine as I realized that something was getting closer to me. I threw my feet onto the floor and quickly reached my light switch to turn on the light. Standing in the middle of the room now, I stared at the wall by my bed, wondering what could be making the noise. I waited to see if it would keep knocking, but it stopped.

"That was weird," I said audibly to myself.

I flipped the light switch off and hesitatingly crawled back into bed. For a few seconds, everything remained quiet and I began to hope for a good night's sleep. That hope faded quickly. Sure enough, just as I pulled the bedspread over my shoulders, the knocking began again, only back at the closet. *Knock, knock. Knock, knock. Knock, knock.* It moved up the wall toward me every few seconds, but I resolved to stay my ground. With each knocking sequence, that resolve faded a bit more until the chills running up my spine overcame it completely. I let it reach my hip level before I jumped up and turned on the light. Once again, it stopped.

One more time, I tested it. I let it reach my shoulders and a chill went up my spine as I cleared the bed in record time to get to the light.

Now I was upset. Something invisible was obviously playing with me. I had read scary stories before about such events, but I never realized just how scary something like this could really be. I stared at the wall, now in anger. I had a science test the next day and I had to get some sleep. I refused to sleep with the light on so I thought maybe the light from the hall would keep it from knocking.

I took a deep breath in relief when I realized that it had worked. I discovered that either turning on the bedroom light or leaving the bedroom door open would inhibit the knocking. I slept with my door open. This worked for me for several months, until my sister got a new dog.

My sister adored her new French Poodle. I hated him. I called him a French Puddle because he thought my room was his personal bathroom. Now I could not leave my door open without being awakened in the middle of the night by the strong smell of dog poop.

So, I tried it again. I closed the door and turned off the light, hoping that whatever it was had left. Once again, the infernal knocking began and crept menacingly toward me on the wall. I already knew how this would go, so I begrudgingly got out of bed and turned on the light.

"Okay! I have had enough! You know what? Go ahead! Knock on the wall all night long! Knock away! I don't care! I'm going to sleep!"

I slid under the blanket and waited. *Knock, knock.* Once again, it crept toward me a few inches at a time. It reached my hip level and I turned away from it to my side. I refused to leave. *Knock, knock. Knock, knock.* It continued until it reached my head level and I put my pillow over my head so I would not hear it anymore.

Then, something knocked pretty forcefully on my pillow twice, right in rhythm. I let out a scream and flew out of bed to turn the light on. I stood there shivering with the sudden realization that whatever it was could actually touch me. My parents, awakened by the racket, ran to my room to see what was wrong. My voice shook as I started to explain what had happened, but when I told them what happened, they did not really believe me. They looked at each other and then back at me with a look that said it all. Finally, they decided to leave me alone with my little problem.

"Go back to sleep. It's just your imagination."

The next day, they tried to explain it away. They told me they thought it was pipes in the wall. Then we found the house plans which proved there were no pipes in that wall. I stood there looking at them in the hope that they would believe me. I could tell that they were not sure what to do with me. I realized that I was on my own, because I was the only one experiencing it and hearing the noise. Finally, I built a barrier against the dog with a large box at my door and left the door open at night and it never happened again.

Still, I knew there had to be something to it, so I began to ask the neighbors if they had heard anything strange about the house.

"The people who had the house before you had a housekeeper who refused to mop the dining room. I remember that it really angered them because they said it was just an excuse not to mop there," answered one neighbor.

"Why did the housekeeper say she would not mop there?"

"She said that a hot hand touched her shoulder every time she got near the wall."

Her statement actually shocked me. My bed rested up against the other side of the same wall the housekeeper was talking about. That meant that whatever it was really could touch someone! It was not just me imagining being touched on the pillow.

As I searched around the neighborhood, I found another neighbor who knew another little fact.

"You know, the woman who had the house built actually died of a heart attack. They found her leaning up against the wall in the dining room."

I was completely freaked out. Did the woman who built the house die against the wall and leave something there? Or, did something in that wall reach out and touch her and cause the heart attack? I was truly scared now.

It became obvious to me that I had been dealing with something spiritual. As a new Christian, I knew little about such things. They terrified me, mainly because I could not see them or understand them and I had no idea that something could be done about it. I did not know that Jesus could keep me safe even though I had been taught that he had descended down into Hell and taken the keys. My only option was to pray for safety and that is exactly what I did. Understanding came to me when I was much older.

SAM

As long as the bedroom door was open, I had nothing to fear and I thought all of the confusion was behind me. As it turned out, it was just the beginning.

One night, I woke up sometime after everyone had gone to bed. My sleepy brain grappled with what I was seeing. A beautiful group of glowing lights danced around in my closet, fading and then growing in intensity. The lights were blue, green, red, purple and yellow and they were about one foot in diameter. I cannot fully describe the intensity of the light. Our language has no words to fully describe the colors. The edges rolled and frothed with iridescence. It was like nothing I had ever seen before. I sat up and stared at it in amazement. What could it be? As I relaxed, I decided that it was beautiful and it began to communicate to me. I heard no voices, just understanding. It told me something I did not want to hear. Sam had died.

Sam was my father's Army friend. Our two families had been stationed together in Panama when I was a child. We all loved Sam, and his son,

Mike, was my very first boyfriend. Our families spent many evenings and weekends together and I loved Sam. Now, I was being led to understand that Sam had died.

I knew that could not be possible. He had been sent to Korea and was now due to come home that week. He had just passed a required physical exam with flying colors and was anticipating his return home after being away for a year. We were all looking forward to it.

So, I began to cry with the knowledge that Sam was dead, and we were all going to be so sad. My parents heard me and came to my room to see what was wrong. I collapsed in my Daddy's arms, cried out, "Sam's dead!" and began to sob uncontrollably. My parents looked at each other in confusion and tried to console me.

"No, no...it's just a bad dream. Sam's fine and he's coming home this week," they said.

"No, he's dead. He died last night."

They did their best to correct me, but I knew he was gone. They told me we would talk about it in the morning. That discussion never happened. They received a phone call that morning informing them that Sam had died suddenly of a massive heart attack the night before. My parents never mentioned it to me. They just began to give me strange looks and I knew they were talking about me. I was something they did not understand.

DAD'S ORDERS

A few months passed after Sam's death and nothing else unusual happened. My life was filled with normal eighth grade activities. The end of the school year was swiftly approaching and my mother began to fret over whether or not to sign her teacher's contract for another year. Apparently, my parents were concerned that my father would receive new orders soon that would require us to move, as we did on a regular basis. If my mother signed the contract, she might not be able to get out of it.

I went to bed, but was soon awakened by another set of beautiful lights. I was concerned because they had brought such bad news the last time I saw them. But, they were different this time. This set of lights communicated to me that my father would get new orders for San Antonio on Saturday morning.

The next morning, I happily announced the good news, hoping it would help relieve some of the tension about signing the contract. It was Wednesday.

"Guess what! You don't have to worry about signing that contract, Mom. Dad is getting orders to move to San Antonio. You will find out on Saturday."

I did not get the reaction I expected. They just looked at me and then at each other. They looked worried, not relieved. I understand that now. I was very sure of my information because I saw it. They did not have that luxury because they did not see it. Nor had they been raised with the experience of the gift of prophecy. It is much easier to believe what you have actually experienced yourself.

So, Saturday came. I usually slept late on Saturdays but I did not want to miss the phone call. I got up and ambled straight into the living room, smiling as I combed my hair. My parents had been acting weird since my announcement. I was sure they would be happy when it actually happened.

I clearly remember that I was sitting with my legs curled up under me on the couch when the phone rang. My parents exchanged glances and then looked at me. My father answered the phone.

"Yes, Sir. Yes, Sir. San Antonio. Yes, Sir."

I was ecstatic. "See? I told you! Now you don't have to worry about it anymore."

Once again I did not get the response I thought I would get. My parents were sure that my prediction would not happen because they could not imagine anyone working on Saturday to inform him of his orders. When the prediction did come true, they had to confess that it was not some lucky guess.

"How did you know this was going to happen?"

"The lights told me. At first, I was afraid they were going to tell me something bad like when Sam died. But God must have heard our prayers. They wanted you to know what to do."

They were very concerned. I, of course, was ecstatic when I realized that the lights could give me good news as well as bad news. I knew my gift was spiritual and trusted it. My parents did not.

Within a month, the Pastor of our church showed up mysteriously at our house…to visit with me. I thought that it was a little strange, but we had a good visit. He asked me questions and seemed satisfied with my answers. I believe he reassured my parents that I was not crazy or possessed. I did not realize any of this until I was much older.

MEDICAL MUSEUM

We moved to Fort Sam Houston in San Antonio that year. I was beginning the ninth grade at a school where, once again, I knew no one. Weekends became a chore because I struggled to find something to do. I had no school obligations because I had not been there long enough. So, I found myself lonely and bored.

We lived in a house that was over one hundred years old. Just around the corner, the Army Medic Corps had established a museum dedicated to Medics through the various wars. I was interested in studying medicine, so I thought I might go check out the old museum.

The museum drew few interested people and, as I entered through the squeaky door, I stepped into another world. The musty smell seemed to fit the items all carefully catalogued in glass display cases. I looked around and found nobody there. And yet, I knew I was not alone. As I perused the cases of antique medic equipment, I could feel someone over my shoulder. This someone, it seemed, was very happy I was there and was very proud. I instantly felt welcomed, like a long-awaited visitor.

It is believed by some that gifted people attract spirits because they are like a shining light or beacon to them. It is as if spirits know when someone can see or feel them. Most people in the world have no ability to sense the spirits or refuse to acknowledge them, so when a gifted person walks into a room, a spirit can hope to be seen or heard.

I was drawn to one particular display from the Korean War. I reached my hand out and lightly stroked the cold glass over the medic equipment and, for some reason, it felt special, like a long-lost friend. Maybe it was special to the spirit who was there with me. I felt like I had made a friend there, so I came back to the museum many times when, as a confused teenager, I felt lonely. I always felt welcome and in the company of someone who appreciated me.

Many years later, I attended a writer's conference where some of the authors were selling their books. One woman had a whole table of books about haunting. She loved the topic of ghosts and had sought out and investigated many reported haunted sites. I decided to visit with her because she and I had something in common. When I told her the story of Mike (I found later the ghost at the museum was named Mike) and how I had come to find him, she got a huge grin on her face.

"Why are you grinning like that?"

"Because I know exactly what medical museum you are talking about. My husband served as the curator of that museum for years."

"Really? Wow. Did you know it was haunted?"

"Oh, yes. Every time they sat down at the table there, they left a chair for their invisible friends. Sounds like you adopted one of them."

I was amazed. I was also happy to find someone who had experienced the same phenomenon as I had. I love validation.

GROWTH AND TEMPTATIONS

Finally, I made some friends at my school. One of my friends was much like me in many ways. Leslie and I were both social outcasts and awkward, but we were also both gifted. When we discovered our similarities, we decided to explore them some. We had heard about what was called ESP. She sat across the library from me during Study Hall and, as previously agreed, we played the ESP game. For ten minutes I would concentrate on "sending" pictures to her. I would write down what I had sent and she wrote down what she "saw." It was fun and very exciting when we saw that I could send things to her and she could send things to me.

"Hey, do you suppose we could send things to other kids?" she suggested one day.

"Okay, but how are we going to know that they got it?"

"We can send something to them that will make them do something they would not normally do."

"Great! Let's try it."

"Let's make Susan do something."

"Like what?"
"Like, uhm, throw her pencil across the room."

As Study Hall began, we both concentrated on Susan and making her want to throw her pencil across the room. She began to look agitated and she rubbed her temples. She picked up her pencil and looked at it strangely. Then, she threw it across the room! As the teacher gave her a glare, we looked at each other with our jaws dropping and stifled our intense desire to laugh.

After that success, we decided that we would try another person.

"Let's see if we can get Wes to crumple his homework paper."
"Good idea!"

Once again, we concentrated on our victim with our directing suggestion. Once again, it worked. Wes stopped working on his English theme paper and then he grabbed it and crumpled it into a tight ball. He immediately picked it back up and carefully unfolded it in confusion. We looked at each other from across the room and ducked our heads, trying to look like we were working as Wes scanned the room. We loved our newly discovered game that saved us from complete boredom in Study Hall.

I began to wonder if I could influence someone to do what I wanted without Leslie's help. So, as I stood outside a store waiting for mother, I decided to try it. A woman stood looking through a display of scarves. I noticed one particularly ugly scarf. The woman had already picked it up and thrown it aside. So, I concentrated on her to make her choose that ugly scarf. After a few moments, she got a confused look on her face, picked up the ugly scarf and went inside to buy it. She then stepped out of the store, took the scarf out of the bag, looked at it and made an irritated expression.

    Suddenly, I realized what I had just done. I had taken a gift that God had given to me and used it in a way I knew He would not approve. That evening, I asked God's forgiveness in Jesus' name and I prayed that He would only let me have or do what He wanted me to have or do. He has honored my prayer. I know now that the enemy loves to tempt God's gifted to use their gifts for evil. I will cite more examples later. That is one reason I have written this book. Hopefully, I can warn others and they can avoid falling for these temptations.

GOOD-BYE FROM A FRIEND

Shortly after my revelation, a tragedy occurred among our friends. My sister's friend became ill with some sort of flu, we thought. It turned out to be spinal meningitis. After a brief struggle with the disease, she died and everyone at the school grieved for her.

The night before the scheduled funeral, my sister and I went to bed, but my sister was so upset she decided to sleep with me in my room. Sometime in the middle of the night, the room grew very cold and I woke up pulling the blanket over me. As I turned onto my back, I realized that the lighting in the room was wrong. Suddenly, I saw her.

She stood at the foot of the bed bathed in a glowing light. She smiled as she extended her arms toward us. I just stopped breathing as I watched her looking sweetly at my sister. She looked at me and said, "Tell her I said good-bye," then she slowly faded away and the light left with her. I started crying and reached for my sister to shake her awake.

She turned to me and said, "What?" I could not speak for a moment and I kept staring at the place where the ghost had stood. Finally, I turned to my sister.

"She was there....right there at the foot of the bed."

"Who?"

"Stacey"

"What do you mean? You know she's dead. Why are you doing this to me?"

"She told me to tell you good-bye."

Her mouth dropped open and she stared at me, then she glanced to the foot of the bed. "How is that possible?"

"I don't know. That's just what she said. She just wanted to see you one last time I guess."

My sister broke down crying. "I'm going to miss her so much." I held her as she sobbed in her grief. The next day, we went to Stacey's funeral with all the rest of her friends and family. As we stood visiting after the service, one of her other friends started crying.

"She came to see me last night."

Another friend said, "Me, too".

We all looked at each other in wonder. Stacey had not been able to say good-bye to her friends before she died, so she visited each one afterwards. I knew I had many things to learn, especially in this area.

CALL TO PRAYER

My mother and two of her sisters all decided that they and all of us cousins would go to Washington, DC, for a vacation in the summer of my freshman year in high school. My cousins and I were all excited and we happily boarded the plane to start our adventure.

We visited a few of the usual tourist magnets each day and one of them was the Congressional Building. Riding from building to building on the underground tram added to the fun of the exploration. We found the cafeteria under Congress and ate there several times, especially since the food was cheaper there. One particular meal became especially exciting.

As usual, I waited in the line and took a tray to get my food. I loaded it with all my favorites and turned to walk to the table where everyone else in our party was sitting. As I turned, my tray picked itself up out of my hands and threw itself across the room! As soon as it crash-landed on the floor and everybody was staring at me, these words came out of my mouth.

"The plane is going to crash."

I did not think those words. It was as much of a surprise to me as it was to everyone else. They all stopped eating and stared at me. I was so embarrassed. And what was that about the plane crashing? My mother said, "What?"

I shook my head with my mouth agape. "I don't know."

Now all of my family was staring at me like I must be crazy. I picked up all my stuff and traded it for a new tray, but I was not hungry anymore. I did not understand what had just happened and I felt so out of control. It was so strange. That tray just picked itself up and threw itself out of my hands. I had not tripped or dropped it. It had a mind of its own. I was so confused and embarrassed.

By now, my mother had become somewhat accustomed to my strange episodes. In fact, she had begun to think that I may well be the next Jean Dixon. Jean Dixon was a famous woman who appeared to be able to predict the future. She had predicted many things accurately, including the assassination of John Kennedy. She had a column with her predictions in every newspaper across the nation.

But I did not feel like I was another Jean Dixon. At that point, I felt like an awkward teenager with an uncanny ability to embarrass myself. Apparently, I did not even have control over my own mouth.

My mother, on the other hand, took my words seriously. She began praying and got my aunts to pray against our return plane crashing. I did not know this at the time.

A few days later, we were at the very same cafeteria....and it happened again! My tray threw itself against the wall, only this time I said, "It's going to be okay." I just wanted to find a rock somewhere and hide under it because I was so embarrassed. I do not believe my cousins have ever thought of me the same again.

My mother was not so sure of my second announcement. When we were getting ready to fly home, she took out the maximum insurance on all of us. I was not afraid. I knew we would be alright, just like my alter ego had said. We boarded the plane for the flight and there was a good deal of turbulence as we crossed the Mississippi River. But we landed in Dallas with no problem.

When we got home, my grandmother called to tell us how fortunate we had been. It seems that a hurricane had headed up the Mississippi River just as we were going to fly across it. The strange thing was, however, that it just stopped moving up long enough for us to cross the river, then proceeded forward.

I learned a few things with all of this. I learned that God did not mind me being embarrassed to get His messages across. I learned that while I was acting in God's service, I did not necessarily have total control over my mouth. I learned that He can call us to prayer when He thinks we need it. And I learned to trust Him. I did not die of embarrassment as I thought I would and He used me to get the rest of the group to pray. I did not know what to think about that at first. Now, when He uses me, I feel so blessed and happy that I do not care what others think about me. I would rather please God any day.

SLUMBER PARTY

My freshman year in high school brought another move. We moved off of Fort Sam Houston and into a big house in the suburbs of San Antonio. The location of the new house required that, once again, we change school districts.

I made a new friend that summer who was a year older than I, and she somewhat adopted me as her own. She introduced me to many new friends and, for the first time in my memory, I began to enjoy myself. I ran with the girls and we had fun. Then, we decided to have a slumber party.

We brought all the usual snacks and records to play and we were well on our way to staying up all night just having fun. After eating pizza for supper, we gathered in Jane's room to play games. At that point, Jane brought out an Ouija Board that she had bought for this occasion. All slumber parties are supposed to include an Ouija Board.

I had never seen or heard of such a device and I was amazed when Jane told us what it could do. We could ask it questions and it would answer them. It did not matter what we wanted to know, the Board could answer it. Jane carefully set out candles on the floor and lit them. Then, she turned off the lights and sat down at the front of the board. So, I watched as the first group of girls put their hands on the planchette and began to ask questions.

"Will Bill ask me to go to the Prom?"

"Will I be able to get into UT?"

"What kind of car will my parents get me for my birthday?"

"Who will I marry?"

The planchette began to slide across the board to answer the questions. The girls began to giggle at the answers and accuse each other of moving it. Everybody denied that they were responsible for its movement.

Then, it was my turn. I sat down and crossed my legs in front of me. Reaching forward, I lightly placed my fingers on the planchette with the others. It came alive under my hand, flying rapidly and repeatedly to "yes." It was no longer sliding slowly around. Instead, it was jerking quickly to the different letters and answers.

"You're moving it!"

"No, I'm not!"

"It wasn't doing that until you touched it."

"I don't know why it's doing that. I am just touching it."

"Oh, sure!" Everybody looked at me accusingly. I knew I was not moving it and I denied it, but they did not believe me.

"Well, ask it something then."

"Okay...What are the initials of the boy I will marry?" I did not want the board to tell the whole name because I had a secret crush. It swept over to the J and the C. This is not what I wanted to hear. I had a major crush on Jane's brother who was in my class and his initials were not JC. So, I asked again.

"No, really. What are the initials of my future husband?"

It flew back to the J and the C. Years later, I married James Crumley, whom I had not met at the time of the incident. When I stopped playing and someone took my place, the planchette began its slow drifting again. The girls accused me of moving it once again. Then, they asked me, "Are you psychic?"

"Uhm, no."

I vigorously denied it because I did not want to be different. I was having too much fun. Then, Jane, whom I had confided in, chimed in.

"Oh, yes she is! She and her friend used to send messages to each other in Study Hall."

The girls got very excited and began to beg me to do it for them. I looked around at a sea of faces eagerly awaiting my performance. Incorrectly, I thought it would make them like me more if I did what they wanted. So, I volunteered to try to make an object move without touching it.

This was one of the skills that Leslie and I had practiced. I picked an object on the fireplace mantle and I told them to watch it. It was a small figurine of a little girl. The room grew quiet as I closed my eyes and concentrated on the figurine. All the girls eagerly watched the figurine. I knew I had done it when they all screamed at the same time and the figurine fell off the mantle to the floor.

Once again, I did not get the reaction I thought I would get. Instead of applauding my talent, they stood around me just staring at me. I knew immediately that I had just committed teenage popularity suicide. It was the same look my cousins had given me when I had pronounced that the plane was going to crash. Over the next few weeks, my friends stopped calling me and inviting me to go with them. My only hope was that my new school was very big and I would be able to find other friends who did not know about me. I certainly would never show off again or even confess my gift without caution. I would have to hide that part of my life from everyone. And, I did for many years.

I told my mother about the Ouija Board at the party. She thought I had enjoyed it so she bought me one and there it sat on my bed when I came home one day. I was very cautious but also very curious about it. Would it still fly around without all the girls helping? I enlisted my sister to play along.

We sat on my bedroom floor and placed our hands on the planchette. Again it seemed to jump when I put my hands on it. Then, it repeated the "yes" behavior it had shown at the party. My sister was amazed. We began to ask questions. At first, it was fun. My sister was excited to ask all the typical teenage questions and find answers to all of life's questions. Then, I started wondering about how all of this worked and started asking more difficult questions.

"What is your name?"
"Mike"
"Are you a spirit?"
"Yes."
"How old were you when you died?"
"Nineteen."
"How did you die?"

"Killed in Korean War."
"What did you do?"
"Medic."
"How did you get put into the board?"

The planchette began to fly around. "Quit asking."

"Are you in Heaven?"
"Quit asking!"
"Are you in Hell?"
"Quit asking!"

It spelled it out over and over and so fast that I was having a hard time keeping my hands on it. My sister yelled at me, "You're doing that, I know it!"

"No, I'm not."
"Yes you are, cuz I'm not doing it."
"No, I'm not!"

At that moment, my sister, who was sitting against a wall, screamed, "Ouch!"

"What?"
"Something just stuck me in my back!"
"No, it didn't."

She rubbed her back, "Yes, look!"

She turned around and pulled her shirt up. There, in the middle of her back, was a small hole bleeding actively. My jaw dropped.

"Can you see it?"
"Yeah…it's bleeding."
"No…"
"Yes."

She turned around and we looked at each other, then back at the board. We ran out of the door to my room and went to get my mother. Neither one of us would pick up the Ouija Board. We refused to touch it. My mother took it and I do not know what she did with it. The board left our lives...but Mike did not.

MIKE

I have heard theories about Ouija Boards. Some say that they can be a portal to the spirit world and that, if a board is destroyed, the portal is closed. Whatever spirits came out of the portal are then trapped here in our existence. I do not know what to think about all of this. I hate to think that Mike was forced to stay with us because of our destruction of the board. I do not even know if it was destroyed. I would prefer to think that Mike stayed with us because he wanted to. All I know is that he stayed.

There are many beliefs about ghosts. In my experience, I know they are real. It is easy to believe in things that you personally see. I can understand why others do not believe in ghosts. It is extremely difficult to believe in things you have never experienced. People also fear things they cannot understand. I do not fear ghosts now.

Is a belief that ghosts exist contradictory to my belief in God? I am quite sure that these beliefs are not mutually exclusive of each other. Many Christians simply refuse to accept that such things are possible. The Bible does not mention ghosts in abundance, but it does talk about them. Paul writes a few verses about visiting with someone he was not sure existed in this world. Paul, being in the Spirit, talks to a ghost. What that tells me is that his spiritual realm included ghosts. He spoke rather like it was a matter of fact. Until I saw those verses, I was conflicted about the things I experienced. Now, I am not.

I have even thought that Mike had been with us already. I knew that I had found a friend at the Medic Museum. I was not aware at the time that he followed me home, but, looking back now, I believe he might have. That would mean that Mike simply used the board to communicate with us. I never felt threatened by Mike and I do not believe that he was responsible for the hole in my sister's back. I feel that Mike was trying to warn us. At any rate, Mike made himself known around the house after the board event. And, it turned out that Mike was quite the prankster.

At first, his actions really scared us. I think he may have gotten some great joy at our teenaged screaming. But, after many years of living with Mike, we realized that he never hurt us and we began to even talk to him when he pulled his stunts.

I have to admit that he scared us badly one night. We were getting ready for bed and the process involved bathing and brushing our teeth in our bathroom. My sister and I were both standing at the double sink in our bathroom when the cabinet door behind us opened slowly. We stopped mid brush stroke and stared into the mirror at the moving cabinet door. Looking at each other, we turned around to face the cabinet, which was three feet away. As soon as the cabinet door opened as far as it could, it suddenly slammed hard and fast. This sent us screaming out of the bathroom, toothbrushes still in hand, down the stairs to our parents. Of course, they did not believe us. After that, we went to the restroom in pairs and kept our eyes glued on the cabinet door. It never happened again.

But, Mike apparently harbored many avenues of entertainment. One of his favorite jokes was to move and hide things from us. For example, I put down my deodorant on the bed. I walked out of the room. I returned to find that the deodorant was not on my bed. I clearly remembered putting the deodorant on the bed so I figured it must have fallen off or something. I pulled the bed skirt up and looked under the bed, but I did not find it. So, I thought maybe I had carried it to the bathroom. I walked to the bathroom to find that I had not left it there. I returned to the bedroom to find the deodorant right where I had left it on the bed. Now, I knew I had not moved it and I knew nobody else was in the house. So, I spoke to the air.

"Mike, stop it! I don't have time for this!"

And, somehow I knew that Mike was there laughing at me. This same joke happened over and over again and everyone in the house became a target. I grew up and left the house and Mike continued his pranks. If one of us was sitting downstairs and nobody was upstairs, we continually heard his footsteps up and down the hallway and into my bedroom.

I think Mike must have followed me around wherever I went. At one point, I visited my grandmother's house and many of my cousins were there. We gathered for a group picture. My grandmother used a Polaroid camera so we waited to see what the picture looked like. There, in the middle of the group and right next to me, was the foggy form of a man. My cousins thought that was very strange, so we took another picture. This time, I moved to the outside of the group. The foggy form moved right along with me. My cousins never really thought about it twice, but I knew what it was. It was Mike.

After we grew up, my sister and I would come home for a visit and Mike would make himself known with his pranks. I remember being very angry with him one day as we were running late to catch a flight and he decided to hide the shoes I was planning to wear. I distinctly remembered placing them on the floor by the bed. When I walked out of the room and returned to put them on, they were gone. I could not find them, so I called my sister to help me. We looked everywhere, including under the bed. When we both walked out of the room and came back, there they were, by the bed where I had left them. We both scolded Mike that time.

Mike liked to mess with my sister's dog. She had a Boston Terrier named Bouncer. Bouncer travelled with her to my parent's house often. On one such visit, Mike played games with Bouncer. My sister was asleep upstairs with Bouncer at her feet. Suddenly, he leapt up and began barking fiercely. He jumped off the bed and ran down the hallway to my bedroom, where Mike slammed the door in his poor face. My sister heard this and got up to investigate. She found Bouncer standing in front of my door, throwing himself against the door and barking ferociously. She opened the door and looked in to find nobody there. But, poor Bouncer spent the rest of the visit walking down the hallway and cautiously standing at my door, looking carefully into the room. He would then turn and walk away, looking back every few seconds.

My parents eventually chose to sell the house and move to a smaller place. The last time I visited the house was the day my father sold it. I stood outside looking up at the windows with my sister and realized that I just had to go back in again, at least one more time.

"I have to go the bathroom. I'll be right back out."

I walked through the door and went up the stairs to the room I had called mine for the last forty years, even though I had not lived at home for at least thirty years. I could feel Mike's presence in the room with me and I realized that I had not explained all of the recent activity to him.

"Mike, I know you're here. I guess you've figured out that we are leaving the house. I want you to know that you are welcome to come live with me at my house if you want to. I understand now. I think I get it. You are and always have been my friend...though your pranks could be a little unnerving. You were probably just trying to entertain yourself. If you decide to stay, there will be a new family to entertain you. They do have four little boys. Just take it easy on them. They might not understand you like we do. I've grown quite used to you and if you do not come home with me, I will miss you. Anyway, good-bye Mike....in case you stay."

I turned around and left the room, stepping down the staircase slowly. I took a deep breath and put a smile on my face as I opened the front door to exit.

"You ready?" my sister asked.

"Yeah, I guess. It's been a good forty years in this house. I'll miss it. And I worry about Mike."

"Oh, yes...Mike. I forgot about him. What is he going to do without us there?"

"I invited him to come live with me."

"Good."

I thought maybe he would enjoy living with a family that had four boys, but he apparently took me up on my offer to live with me. Mike occasionally makes himself known at my present house. He still moves things. In one instance, he helped me. I had gone through my crowded bedroom with an armful of laundry on my way to the laundry room. As I passed my dresser, a corner of the sheets knocked a bottle of fingernail polish to the floor. I noticed it, but continued on my way intending to pick it up as I came back through. When I came back, however, the bottle of polish was sitting back up on the dresser.

"Thanks Mike! I see you decided to stay with me. You are welcome...just behave yourself and don't scare my grandkids." I knew it was Mike using his talents to help me. I still feel his presence at my home and it is not frightening. It is more like having a friend with me all the time.

At one point, I thought I had figured out Mike's exact identity. I met a friend of James' family named Betty at a restaurant one day and James and I sat and visited with her for a good while. James had an uncle named Clinton whom I had never met. But apparently Betty had known Clinton and she spoke of him almost like she had harbored a crush on him when she was younger. Clinton had run around with her big brother. As I sat and listened to the conversation, I became very interested in some of the things I learned.

Apparently, Clinton had served as a medic in Korea. I asked how old he was when he was killed.

"He was nineteen," was her answer.

This sounded very familiar and I instantly thought of Mike. Mike was a medic killed in Korea at the age of nineteen. But, I knew that I was dealing with someone named Mike, not Clinton. Still, I asked what Clinton's middle name was. Maybe it was Michael. James did not know. That night I dreamed a dream in color. When my dreams are in color, I pay attention because they often become real. Mike introduced himself and I saw his face and heard his voice for the first time. He smiled at me and shook his head.

"Not Clinton," was all he said.

The voice and face were not at all what I had expected Mike to have. I could see the jolly nature in his eyes as he laughed at me trying to figure out who he was. Somehow, however, I got the real impression that he had known Clinton.

THE GIFT BEGINS TO MATURE - DISEMBODIED TRAVELING

My Junior Year in High School began and I dated a boy named Robert. Robert treated me like a queen and constantly showered me with gifts, flowers and attention. I was not sure how I felt about him, but he certainly was trying hard.

One weekend, my parents decided we should all go visit my aunt and uncle in Wichita Falls. I was excited because these cousins were always entertaining. The four-hour trip got us there just in time for supper. We visited some and then all went to bed.

I dreamed the strangest dream. It was all in color, which I have now learned means it was not just a dream. I dreamed that I flew (not in a plane) back to San Antonio and found Robert. He was driving to the Mall and I was with him, only he did not know it. He parked his car in the parking garage next to a department store and opened the door to go in. I was trying to follow him, so I had to stay up close because he did not know I was there and he did not hold the door open for me.

He walked in and went up to the candy department of the store. Choosing carefully, he bought a little stuffed bunny with a bag of chocolate candy attached. The bunny was wearing a little hat with pink flowers on it and had a belt made of the same material. The clerk who sold it to him was a blonde teenager who was very friendly. "Your girlfriend sure is lucky!" I remember her saying. He shopped around and looked at clothes, buying a pair of blue running shorts for himself. Then, he left the store and went home. I then flew back to Wichita Falls.

I woke up the next morning and told my sister about the weird dream.

"It was so funny! I had my arms spread out like a plane and I was dipping in and out of the clouds. I really enjoyed it but the landing was a little rough. I woke up catching my breath like I had fallen off a tall tree or something."

When we got back to San Antonio, Robert came to see me...and brought me the same little bunny I had seen in my dream. I guess my jaw dropped a little and I looked confused.

"What's wrong?"

I hesitated, "Uhhh...I'm not sure."

"Well, what?"

I began to tell him about my dream. I included every little description of his shopping trip. Now it was his turn to drop his jaw.

"How did you do that?"

"I...don't know."

I was somewhat afraid of his reaction, but he seemed to be able to take it all in without too much difficulty. He was just amazed and thought it was cool. I have since had relationships with other people who were not so cool with it. They either choose to disbelieve me or simply ignore it. It is something they do not understand and they do not know what to do with it.

TMI

As the year passed, I noticed another quirk of the gift. This is one part of the gift that I do not particularly like. I can read people.

The first time I noticed it was when one of my friends had a cousin come to visit. We had all gotten together on a Saturday night when we were introduced. Instantly, everyone liked him. Instantly, I did not. I did not know why I had an instant distrust of him, but I did. Everyone else was smiling and being friendly to him, but I was hanging back watching every move. I just knew that he could not be trusted.

It was not long before my other friend started dating him.

"I don't know…I just don't like him," I told her.

"Why?"

"I just feel like you can't trust him for some reason."

"Oh, you're just being silly. He hasn't done anything wrong and he's really cute."

"I'm telling you that he's bad news. Be careful."

I worried about my friend and I did not know why. A nagging feeling bothered me when I thought about him. But my friend ignored my warning and just laughed at me. Within a month, they were going steady and my distrust became a sticking point between us.

At that time, I got a job working at a movie theater selling tickets. As the movies were about to begin, a long line would form at the window. One evening, I looked up to see my friend's steady boyfriend in line with another girl. They were flirting with each other and she was wearing his senior ring. He did not realize I was there until he got up to the window and he suddenly turned pale when he saw me. I just smiled at him and sold him his tickets. As soon as I got a chance, I phoned my friend and asked if they had broken up or something of which I was not aware. She told me that they were better than ever.

"I need to tell you something."

"What?"

"He came to the movie last night and I sold tickets to him."

"Tickets?"

"Yes, tickets...as in multiple...as in two."

"Why did he buy two tickets?"

"He bought one for the girl who was with him."

"What girl?"

"I don't know. But she had his ring on her finger."

"What?!"

"Call him and ask him about it."

She called him and found out that he was also going steady with a girl from another school. She quickly broke up with him.

This incident was just the beginning of this part of the gift. It progressed. Soon, I would see flashes of things when I was around someone. Many times, they were good things that I saw but many times they were not. I never really knew what to do with all of that information. I did my best to not let it affect my relations with people, but sometimes it did. I had no proof of anything I was seeing at the time. I would have thought that I was just losing it, but sometimes I got confirmation of some of the most outrageous visions. I still have problems with this aspect of my gift, but my family has learned to listen when I have alarm bells about someone.

As I have lived with this, I know that it is information that God wants me to know for some reason. The gift has a name in the Bible...Gift of Discernment. It has kept me safe many times and God had also used it to help others.

Much later in my life, I was walking down a mall and a strange man began to follow me. He looked quite normal physically. I did not want to have anything to do with him because alarm bells were going off about him and I saw some really awful flashes. Suddenly, I heard an audible voice.

"Stop. Sit down on that bench."

I argued, "What?! That man is dangerous."

I heard it again, so I stopped and sat down on the bench, having learned to listen when God uses an audible voice. Immediately, he sat down next to me. Then I heard, "Tell him that I love him."

In my head, I argued again, "Everybody knows that you love them."

"Tell him that I love him."

So, I turned to him and said, "God wants me to give you a message. He says He loves you."

The man's face contorted as he began to weep. "You don't understand...God can't love me...I'm too evil...I've done so many bad things...He can't love me."

"I don't know about all of that but He told me to tell you He loves you."

The man broke down and began to sob. I told him to talk to God, confess his sins and ask for forgiveness in the Name of Jesus Christ. Then, I got up and walked away, leaving him in the arms of the Holy Spirit. As I left, I heard the words I crave, "Well done, my daughter."

In my teaching career, I saw many flashes with many students. They served to help me help my students in ways besides teaching science. I am always so happy when God uses me like that.

NO SECRETS

When I was in my Senior year in High School, the Army decided to send my father to California to attend language school and learn Japanese. Once again, I found myself in the situation of having to leave my school with my family. This time it was different, however, because my parents had purchased our house in San Antonio, in the plan of eventually retiring there. As they considered their options, my parents realized that the language school would only take six months and it would be much better if my mother stayed with us in San Antonio while my father went to California. So, once again he kissed us all good-bye and left on a plane.

One night, I dreamed again in color. This time, in my dream, I was me, but not me. An ambulance came and picked me up to transport me to the hospital. They checked me out and told me that I had had a minor stroke but I would be alright. Then, they told me I could go home. I woke up saying, "Great, but you guys brought me here and I don't have my car. How am I supposed to get home?"

I got out of bed and called my mother. "Mom, did someone have a stroke?"

"No, not that I know of. Why?"

"Because I had a dream in color again and I dreamed that somebody had a stroke. They are okay, but they had to find a way back home from the hospital."

"Well, I don't know of anyone. I'll keep my ears open though."

I continued to ask around because the dream was in color, but never figured out who it was. A year later, when my father came home from California, he confessed that he had suffered a stroke right at the time I had the dream. He had not told us about it because it was an extremely small stroke and he did not want us to worry. He laughed and said he could not figure out how to get home because the ambulance had brought him there to the hospital and left him there. Mystery solved.

LOVE AND FAMILY - TRUTH IN CONFESSION

Romance found me my first year in college. I dated a boy from New Mexico named Don for the entire year and, when summer came, he went back home to work.

We wrote letters to each other as we could not afford long distance phone calls. Before he left, we decided to go out with others so we would not be bored. I went out with many different boys. He went out with one girl.

Well, we all know how that works. Of course, he did not mention this aspect of his summer to me in his letters. I sat at my house pining over him and telling myself how much I loved him. I guess God decided that I needed to know the truth.

Night after night, I dreamed about Don. I remember that the dreams were odd in that they were in color. Also, it was as if we were meeting in real time.

In the dreams, we met in the Commons, the cafeteria at the college we attended together, only it was always night. The chairs rested upside down on the tables, the lights were turned off and there was nobody else there. We discussed everything about our day, even mundane things. I told him about the clothes I had modeled that day and the people I had met selling tickets at the theater that night. He told me about his summer job...... and Debra. Debra did this and Debra did that. I knew all about Debra. I knew her full name, where she lived, what her house looked like, her work for the summer, the car she drove and all about her family. He freely related to me every interesting tidbit about Debra.

This went on nightly for several weeks. In the meantime, he wrote a few letters to me about his summer. None of his letters mentioned anyone named Debra but I knew something was going on. Finally, one dream confirmed what I was beginning to believe.

In the dream, Don and I got married. We went through the whole ceremony and reception, and Debra followed us everywhere. I was sure that she would go away now that Don and I were married. No. She followed us on our honeymoon and even to our honeymoon suite.

Well, I may be slow, but I finally got it. God was trying to tell me that Don was not to be mine. He was apparently to marry Debra. I would be finding someone else.

At first it upset me greatly. After a while though, I realized that God was sparing me from a lot of grief. I gradually accepted it and decided to go on with my life without Don. I stopped pining away about missing Don and I stopped dreaming about him.

Within two weeks, we returned to college and I readied myself for the inevitable discussion. I went to his place and held him tight, then backed away from him.

"What's wrong?" he asked.

"We have to talk."

"Okay. What?"

"I have decided to break up with you."

Don's expression changed from humor to concern. "Why?"

"You are going to marry Debra and I am marrying someone else."

"Debra? What do you know about Debra?"

"Everything."

"Like?"

I began to tell him everything about Debra. I included every aspect that he had disclosed to me in my dreams. He just stared at me.

"How did you know all that? Did you hire a detective?"

"No. You told me."

"Huh? I did not! How did you know all that?"

I told him about my nightly dreams where he told me everything. I described the whole setting to him, including the description of the Commons at night. I mentioned each detail about his work that he had shared with me. Then, I explained the dream about our wedding and honeymoon with Debra following along.

"You are supposed to marry Debra, not me."

I gathered up my things and left the room. As I recall, he never tried to discount any of the things I told him. I never went out with him again. And, yes, he did marry Debra. I was never sad about losing him. God had shown me that He had someone else for me and I had faith that He would lead me to him. And it did not take long.

LIFE GOES ON

Within a few months, I had found James, my future husband. Our romance blossomed and we planned to marry after we finished school. God sent me a dream in color again to assure me that this would happen sooner than that, before we finished school.

My father's favorite pastime was trading cars. He constantly shopped around, even when he had just purchased a new vehicle. At the time, he had just bought a beautiful Buick LeSabre with the most luxurious seats. Before he had even bought this car, I had the dream.

In the dream, I was sitting in this car (which I had never seen before) on the way to my wedding with James. Imagine my excitement when my parents first showed me their new car. It was the car that would take me to my wedding and I knew it would be soon because of my father's trading habits. The very next year, that car carried me to the church and I married James.

Life continued at a faster pace now as we both finished school and went to work. We decided not to have children at first so we could travel around for a while. Finally, the urge to have a baby hit me hard. I began to beg James and he agreed. The only problem was that I had been on birth control for five years and pregnancy eluded me for quite a while.

Out of desperation, I cried out to God. "Oh God, please let me have a baby...when will I get pregnant?" I got my answer that night.

Standing in the far corner of our bedroom stood a man. He was an adult but, as he walked closer to me, he became younger. By the time he reached my bedside, he was a baby. Then, he tried to jump into my belly! I freaked out and he disappeared. Within a few seconds, the man stood back in the same corner of the room as before. He walked toward me, again losing age as he approached until he became a baby. Again, he tried to jump into my belly. Again, I freaked out and he returned to the corner as a man. Finally, on the third try, I relaxed and he managed to get into my belly. Then, I awoke. Weird dream! I fully described it to James and told him what our son would look and be like.

The dream showed me three different attempts and exactly three months later I became pregnant with my son. The truly remarkable thing is that, as an adult, he looks exactly like the man I saw in the corner of my room. God had answered my question. Not only did He tell me it would be another three months, but He showed me what my son would look like. God is just SO WONDERFUL!

CONNECTIONS

One morning, as I lay in bed thinking about getting up, I heard a voice. The voice said, "Karen!" It did not sound like James, but I rolled over and said, "What?" James opened his eyes and looked at me with a confused look on his face.
"I didn't say anything."
"Yes you did. You said my name."
Now he began to get agitated. "No, I didn't!"
Okay... I just rolled back over and tried to go back to sleep. A few seconds later I heard it again, only this time I realized that it was not James' voice. It was my Dad's voice. Nobody says my name like he does. It had to be my Dad, but my Dad was three hours away from me.

Now, I became concerned. I remembered the stroke incident and got up to dial his number. It was busy. I tried again and it was still busy. I kept trying until he, at last, answered the phone. Anguish filled his voice. He had just received a call from one of his brothers that his other brother had died suddenly. The reason I could not get through to him was now clear. The reason I was to call him was also now clear. I talked to him for quite a while and tried my best to comfort him as much as I could. God had just helped me love my Dad a little more.

I have come to know that God does this a lot. Many instances of my gift have been used to comfort others. This was just one of the first opportunities.

Returning to teaching after the birth of my son was extremely difficult for me. I hated leaving my son at the babysitter, knowing I could not be with him like I wanted to be. Still, it had to be done because of our finances. So, I begrudgingly returned to the classroom.

One morning, as I stood teaching Biology class, I suddenly was overwhelmed! In a huge flash, I saw a face up close and I panicked. To the class, it appeared that I had just stopped talking in the middle of a sentence and stared forward for a few seconds. When I mentally returned to the classroom, I realized that all of my students were just staring at me. I had not snagged their attention that well ever before. They sat watching me in some sort of anticipation. I stammered.

"Oh, uh, sorry....I just remembered something," I said as I attempted to get myself out of another embarrassing situation. I said a silent prayer and asked God to protect whoever was involved with that vision. Then, I just went on with the lesson. What else could I do? I had no idea what that vision had been about or who it involved.

This was just the first of many such incidents in my life. I have learned that I do not have to know what is really going on because God does. He is in charge and all He wants me to do at that point is to pray for whoever is involved. I may or may not get to discover an explanation of the vision. It is all up to God. However, this particular vision was soon to be explained.

I drove to the babysitter's house to pick up my son after school. I gave a quick knock on the door and walked in, only to come face to face with the person I had seen in the vision. I must have gasped because the boy jumped back a little. Then my babysitter tried to introduce me to him.

"Oh, sorry. This is my nephew, Bill. He came to stay with us for a few days. But, I don't think your son likes him very much. You should have seen the panic fit he threw when Bill tried to pick him up! I think he's okay with him now, though."

I never knew why I saw all of that. The boy was perfectly nice. What I did learn was that my son and I must be connected in a way that I had never known was possible. There have been several instances of this since then, even though he is an adult.

Many years later, my son became a policeman in a large town. Of course, this has kept me on my knees praying for his safety. One particular night, I awoke from a deep sleep and gasped.

"Pray for Josh!" came out of my mouth as I sat up. I glanced at the clock and it read 2:30 in the morning. I knew that he was on duty that night so I just dropped down and began to pray until I felt that everything would be alright. Then, I went back to sleep. The next afternoon, I called him and asked him what he was doing at 2:30 in the morning that I needed to pray about.

"Oh, that was the meth house."

That answered my question. Most law enforcement agencies have a policy against entering a meth house if the smell is strong because of the probability that it will explode. But, when my son approached the house and knocked, a small child answered the door and he became worried about the child. The house reeked of the explosives required to make the drug and he knew it could explode at any time. He ran through the house, opening windows and doors to clear the fumes and he got all the people out of the house. He was in extreme danger. That was why God told me to get on my knees immediately. Thank-you, God, for allowing me to help him. All I know to do is to pray. I guess that is all I am supposed to do.

LONG-TERM VISIONS

We moved to Brackettville, Texas, and I became pregnant with my second son. Shortly after Caleb's birth, a series of dreams overwhelmed me. For three nights in a row, I dreamed in color, again. These dreams did not make much sense, but they were very intense. So, I told James all about them each morning and I clearly remember them even now.

The first night, I dreamed that I was standing in a building close to the only intersection with a red light in Brackettville at the time. It was as if I stepped into some kind of catastrophe shortly after it had happened. Everyone was upset and scared. Shortly, someone walked up to me and asked me questions.

"Is the water okay?" they quizzed.

"I don't know yet. The test results are not ready yet."

"Well, how do we know whether or not it is safe to drink the water yet?"

"You have to wait. The bacteria need at least a day to grow."

I became aware that the catastrophe involved the drinking water somehow. In earning my Microbiology Degree, I had learned about water testing. At the time, a water sample must be plated on agar plates to see if any E. coli would grow. If E. coli grew, it was assumed that the drinking water had fecal contamination and it should not be consumed. Apparently, I was testing the water for bacteria in the dream. That was all I knew.

The second night, I saw my own death. Now, this is not something that is wonderful to see. I was standing in the middle of an intersection with many other concerned people. Something had happened, but I was not aware of what it was.

Suddenly, I looked up to the sky to the West. Someone on a scooter died and then rose back up. The sky turned pink and darker pink clouds were rolling quickly towards us. Everyone panicked and cried out in fear. As the cloud approached, it overcame people that we could see. They went down and died, and then stood back up. I braced for the impact of the cloud. When it hit, I remember it hurt and I went down as I died. A few seconds after that, I stood up and looked around. All of us who had died stood there trying to figure out what had just happened. It was just so fast. Then, I woke up.

By the third night, I was half afraid to go to sleep. It is not every day that you see yourself die. Sure enough, as soon as I fell to sleep, the dream began, again in color. It was me, but not me. I was flying way up above the Earth as I watched what was going on below. I saw an army of tanks rolling out of Saudi Arabia towards Israel. At the top of the lead tank stood a man in a white turban pointing forward with extreme determination on his face. I saw his face plainly, even though I was apparently far above him. Then, I awoke. The man's face was emblazoned in my memory and I can still see it clearly.

All of these dreams occurred in 1980. None of it made any sense. But, I have learned through all of this that, most of the time, it does not. Apparently, I do not need to understand it....God does. What am I supposed to do when I see things like this? First, pray. Then, tell someone...anyone who will listen.

That is the other problem with this "gift." Nobody wants to listen. I do not blame them. If I had not seen it with my own eyes, I would not believe it either. Also, people do not want to know about bad things. They want to go on about their blissfully happy lives not knowing what is coming around the corner. It is just easier that way. I must confess that this series of dreams left me quite unsettled. I had to wonder what they were all about.

After a while, when none of this happened and I did not die, I relaxed about the whole scene. But the awe of it never left me and I watched cautiously how the world unfolded.

MY TURN TO LISTEN

One afternoon, my parents and my sister came to visit us. Clouds began to gather and a storm soon exploded with violent lightning and thunder. James was out working at the ranch at the time and the children were all playing in their rooms.

Suddenly, Josh, then five years old, came screaming out of his room.

"Dad's gonna get hit by lightning!"

We all turned and looked at him. I recognized his predicament. He knew it made no sense to anyone else. But it made sense to me.

"What do you mean?" I asked.

"I saw it," he said, looking around from face to face.

I knew what was needed. "Okay...don't worry....we'll pray right now."

We stopped and said a prayer asking God to protect James. Josh seemed to be happier with that. A few hours later, James came home and the first words he said confirmed what Josh had seen.

"I was almost hit by lightning. All the hair stood up on my body and I heard crackles in the air around me," he continued. Later, as I told him of Josh's pronouncement and our prayer, he said he knew God had saved him there. The lightning nearly killed him, but once again, God called us to prayer. I do not think that He actually needs the prayer. I think, instead, that He wants us to realize that He has saved us because we asked. He always answers prayer in one way or another.

There have been many instances of God using others to tell me things I needed to know. I am sure I do not understand all that I know about this. Why does He not just show me in a dream or tell me in His usual methods? Maybe my life is just too demanding at the time and I am not paying attention. Most of the time, someone will tell me what they dreamed and I will have an instant understanding of it.

ANGELS

God has an army of angels. This is probably not a great revelation to most people. Angels appear in the Bible in multiple stories of God's doings. Even in the Bible, angels are varied in many ways. Sometimes they are seen and sometimes they are invisible. Sometimes they are visible only to certain people in order to accomplish their tasks. Sometimes they look like ordinary people.

I have already mentioned the angel in my room when I was four years old. I plainly saw her and she looked as real as you and me. This proved to be only the first of many. They have always brought comfort and help, usually as a result of prayer.

One such angel appeared to me in a cafeteria located in a mall. God had blessed me with a beautiful daughter three years after the birth of my second son. She was two when I took my three children shopping and we decided to stop for a lunch at the cafeteria there. The children skipped and ran eagerly everywhere we went in the mall and exhaustion began to wear on me as we entered the cafeteria and stood in line. Each kid fought with me about what they would eat and how much they could get. After we paid, we headed to a table in the middle of the room and I struggled to get everybody seated and started with their meals. One child continued an argument started in the line about the desserts and the other two began to chime in with him. The youngest refused to stay in her chair and the two boys began to slap at each other. I began to feel like I could not take another minute of this insanity.

Suddenly, I felt someone watching me and I turned in the direction of the sensation. There, sitting alone in a booth not too far away, sat a man looking at me with the warmest expression. A slight smile and loving eyes met mine. I noticed that he did not have a tray. As I watched him, he closed his eyes and spoke something that I could not hear over the commotion at my table.

Something drew my attention suddenly to my children. It was silence. I could not believe my eyes. The kids were sitting in their chairs eating. They were eating without fighting or carrying on. This stymied me. My children never did this. I stared at them in complete awe. Then, I remembered the man in the booth. I looked back over to where he had been. He was just gone. He did not walk out because he would have had to walk right by me and I would have seen him. He just disappeared. He just appeared, prayed for me and then he just disappeared. The kids were perfect for the rest of the day. I could not explain it, but I surely appreciated it.

Another angel appeared in my living room when I was freaking out over an approaching tornado. I was at home alone. The house we lived in was basically built on railroad ties and did not have a foundation. It lacked the luxury of a good place to hide in a tornado. I could get into a closet, but it would be just like getting into a closet in a trailer. If a tornado decided to pick up the house, it could just toss it around at will.

Darkness crept over the house as the menacing clouds gathered at the edge of an approaching storm. I slipped from window to window to keep my eye on the clouds. They warned of hail with their green shimmer and they included several areas of boiling air. The clouds swirled and churned into a vortex that began to descend from the sky. I freaked out. What could I do? I ran from one end of the living room to the other in panic.

Suddenly, I stopped in my tracks. A man sat on my couch looking at me calmly. I froze and let my jaw drop. He just looked at me.

"Sit down and relax."

I paused for a second in disbelief. How did he get into my house? Who was he? And why was he telling me to sit down and relax? He did not look dangerous. Then, I realized that I might as well sit down and relax because if a tornado came I would be gone regardless of what I did. So, I sat down on the other couch and just stared at him. He looked vaguely familiar. He was short and had dark hair and large eyes. I felt completely comfortable with him. I looked down at my trembling hand and then looked back to the other couch. He was gone.

I just kept going over it in my head. What had just happened? I was freaking out and somebody materialized in my living room and told me to relax. I completely forgot about the storm outside as I rubbed my eyes and kept looking back at the couch.

The storm passed without incident, but I continued to fret over the man. Later, I realized that he looked like someone I had seen before. His face resembled pictures of my grandfather when he was young. Then, I remembered that my grandfather was only five feet three inches tall. Well, no wonder he looked familiar!

I am not sure what I think about all this. I am quite convinced that my grandfather came to me at my moment of pure panic to comfort me. This tells me that he could see what was happening to me and that he was able to bridge the gap between the living and the dead for a few moments to help me out. I cannot describe how much this thought comforts me or why. I am not alone, even in the worst storm....literally.

Many years later, still another angel entered my life and the lives of my daughter and my granddaughter. They appear when we need them the most. They serve and protect us as instructed by God, who responds to our prayers.

My daughter decided to move into her own apartment in San Antonio and she had her one and a half year old daughter with her. I worried incessantly about this. I pictured them alone in an apartment surrounded by people I did not know or trust. So many horrible possibilities presented themselves to my little paranoid brain that had been overfed by watching the San Antonio news. I began to pray and I kept praying with every breath. How could they be safe there?

The day came and we hauled all of her earthly possessions upstairs into her new apartment as all kinds of people watched. You must understand that my daughter is beautiful and tall and I could just feel the evil thoughts of some of the men who were her new neighbors. As we struggled with the last of the furniture up the stairs, I sat down on her rocking chair and held tightly to my grand-daughter, not wanting to leave. They seemed so vulnerable.

I rocked my grandbaby and stalled my departure. Suddenly, Kimberley looked up to the corner of the apartment by the dining area. I looked there too. There was nobody there. She broke a big smile and waved at nothing in the corner.

"Hi!"

My daughter and I exchanged glances. We saw nothing, but Kimberley was very excited to see someone.

A feeling of relief rushed over me. The angel had just arrived and I cannot tell you how I knew that. He was just there and I felt it. Apparently, Kimberley saw him. To shorten the story a little, my daughter kept that angel very busy. Strange coincidences happened all the time that proved that someone was helping her. When her car tire had a blowout, it occurred right in front of the tire shop. When the muffler fell off of her car, it happened right in front of the muffler shop.

One day an armed robber showed up at a car wash where my daughter was washing her car. With his hand in his pocket, he approached her and asked her for some change. She gave some to him. He got a very strange look on his face and then turned away. A few moments later, she looked over and saw that the man had a gun drawn from his pocket as he robbed another customer. Who knows how that angel managed that one? All I know is that she led a charmed life, escaping the usual hazards with what seemed to be help from above. I am convinced that the angel kept her safe. I believe that he is still at work. God is so faithful to us.

BATTLES

Janie lived in a little travel trailer close by our house and she worked at the school. I knew her because of my association with her at school and because I visited her sometimes at her trailer. She had served in the military and now lived alone, happily enjoying her life as a teacher's aide.

One morning, Janie came running over to the house screaming in panic. Frantic door banging forced me to the door quickly.

"Help! Something is attacking me!"

"What?!! What's attacking you?"

"I don't know...my trailer just started jumping all around like we were having an earthquake."

"What? There wasn't an earthquake....we're in Texas!"

"I know, but I swear it bounced around so bad that I fell over and had a hard time getting up."

I just looked at her in disbelief. Her dark eyes darted back and forth in fear and she was shaking. This I had to see.

We walked over to her trailer and I saw nothing out of ordinary as we approached it. But, when we opened the door, the scene told a completely different story. Dishes were tossed off the counter and table and everything looked exactly like somebody had taken that trailer and shaken it around. Little figurines had fallen and moved over. Janie had never been an immaculate housekeeper and dust had obviously built up on her countertops and figurines. The strange thing was that the places where the figurines had been were dust-free. Obviously, they had all been moved.

"Okay, Janie, that's just weird. You're right…it looks like somebody picked up your trailer and shook it around. But, I would have felt it if it had been an earthquake and nothing happened at my house."

As I looked at her, her eyes dropped to the ground. "There's more that you don't know."

"Like what?"

"Like sometimes my bed jumps around all by itself. I know I am not alone in here. I just don't know what to do."

The whole picture began to form in my mind. Janie was under spiritual attack. I stopped and closed my eyes for a few seconds. I could feel it. With my growing spiritual awareness, I knew what to do.

"Come with me. Let's go get James."

We walked back over to my house and explained the whole thing to James. James and I decided to go to Janie's house and pray and do spiritual battle with whatever was scaring Janie. We prayed before we left our house. We prayed for forgiveness of our sin and for God's angels to come and do the actual warfare against the enemy. Then, we went to Janie's house.

James, Janie and I walked through the entire trailer, holding the Bible and praying. The atmosphere changed and became very hot, but we kept it up.

"The Lord rebuke you! Be gone from here! The Captain of the Army of Hosts has taken the keys of Hell and you are now cast down into the pit from which you came, in the Holy name of Jesus. Be gone!" We did this over and over and then prayed for angels to come and protect Janie from any further attacks. Then, we went home.

That night I dreamed the strangest dream. I heard noises coming from my garage and I went to investigate. When I opened the door to the garage, the air changed and I knew that the enemy was there. A set of chains that hung from the ceiling to store the bicycles began to sway for no apparent reason. I began to pray loudly against the enemy and I believe that battle continued throughout the entire night. I was exhausted when I woke up, but I believe I was successful in keeping the enemy from entering our house. Janie never had another problem with her bed or other things moving around.

INEVITABLE CONFLICT

Even though we had found a church that taught more about the Spirit, I never really felt free to expose my full gift. It seemed that the rules of man managed to creep into even the more spiritual congregations. This church we attended claimed to be completely led by the Spirit, but in truth, it was led by a mixture of the Spirit and the beliefs of one man.

I knew what I was seeing. Still, I felt so much more freedom in this group of believers than I had ever felt before so I guarded my tongue in order to keep peace. Another woman in the group shared the gift that I had and we often confirmed our visions with each other. We were free to express our visions as they came and this continued until it became inconvenient for our group leader.

A conflict had arisen between some of the members of the church. Some of the leaders of the group began to think that they were more holy than others. Eventually, this led to a confrontation between the "holy" ones and the "less than holy" ones. The leader was accused of working towards his personal agenda and he adamantly argued against this accusation.

Suddenly, he called on me to ask God what He thought about it. Specifically, he asked me to ask God what He saw in his spirit. He was confident that I would only see purity in his intentions. I believe that he was blinded to his own ambition.

I hesitated because I knew what I had seen many times concerning this question and I knew its revelation would not be taken easily. Slowly, I bowed my head and asked God to show me what He wanted us to know. Sure enough, a creature appeared immediately in my vision. I gasped as I saw it and opened my eyes to see everyone in the group staring at me in wonder.

"Well, what did you see?" our leader asked confidently.

"Are you sure you want me to tell you what I really see?"

His brow creased a little. "Yes, go ahead."

I swallowed hard. "OK then. I saw a many-headed dragon."

Now, it was the group that gasped. I cut my eyes over to the other gifted woman and she just nodded and put her head down.

"Oh, come on!" our leader exclaimed. "You can't believe that!" he yelled to the group. "What does that mean?"

"I am only telling you exactly what I saw. I do not know what it means. Maybe you can tell me."

He stormed from the room and the meeting dissolved. Nothing was ever the same in our group after that. Our leader withdrew further into his "holiness" and would have nothing to do with me or my gifted friend ever again. He basically went about trying to discredit us in every way and refused to confess that there was any truth to the vision. Still, the other members told me that they felt that the vision was correct.

Our little group dissolved before long and we all went back to the various churches from which we had come. The whole experience gave us wisdom and a new perspective on religious beliefs. Man tends to corrupt even the most pure worship with his own essence. Only God is Holy.

Still, I learned much from my experience with the little group. I learned how to pray a little deeper and enter a less distracted state. I learned that Christ will show Himself to us as we enter deep into prayer. There are no words that can describe His eyes. The closest words are intense Love and Light, all mingled into one. His essence is unimaginable to the little box that is our mind. So beautiful!!!

We have been members of several different churches since this episode of my life. I try to blend in with the others as much as possible, rarely mentioning my gift, if at all. I do this to keep peace among the members and, quite frankly, to avoid being ostracized by them. Many people do not understand the gifts of The Spirit and I do not want to offend them. Still, there are times when the gift just slips out.

One such incident occurred when we had a relatively young new pastor. I knew that he and his family were more versed in the Spiritual gifts than other pastors I have followed. His young wife took responsibility for running the choir, of which I was a member. She tended to be a very strong personality usually, but one day she became emotional during practice and walked out on the choir to go hide in her husband's office, crying. We all looked at each other and I got up to pursue her. I knocked on the office door and she told me to come in. I hugged her really hard and just looked at her. Then, once again, words came out of my mouth that I had not thought.

"You are pregnant and it is a girl."

I stepped back from her with my eyes wide. Why did I say that? I had no clue. She immediately burst into laughter. Uh, oh. I was sure I had just lost a friend. Then she grabbed me and hugged me.

"Thank-you! You just confirmed what I thought. I'm two weeks late and I have been so worried that I have not been able to stop thinking about it. I guess it has really been affecting me. How did you know?" She gave me a quizzical look. Now it was my turn to explain.

"I...I...don't know," I answered as I shrugged my shoulders. I looked at her and decided that I might as well confess the truth. "Sometimes my mouth has a mind of its own."

She stopped and looked closely at me. Her mouth came open and then she smiled at me.

"You have the gift of Prophecy. That's what that is. God just used you to give me a message that I desperately needed to hear."

I had never quite heard anyone put my gift in those terms before. It made me feel wonderful. It made me feel normal. It made me feel accepted. She and I became good friends and she gave birth to the cutest little girl eight months later.

EVERYWHERE

The small town we lived near proved to be loaded with spirit opportunity. I suppose every community is likewise loaded. Our small town included an old Army Fort that had been bought by private enterprises. Army Forts are full of spirit activity and I experienced plenty of incidents at this particular Fort.
Part of the Fort had been made into a Senior Center where we could go to work out in a small gym toward the back of the building. My husband and I decided to try it out one day, so we gathered our gym clothes and drove over to the Senior Center.
The old building still had most of its Army post format, but it had been carpeted. Several donated pieces of equipment sat randomly around the room, waiting for us to come use them. I took a look around and saw some that I wanted to use, but I had to go change first. I looked for a bathroom and soon found the tall door leading to the Lady's room. Pushing open the door, I found an unpleasant surprise.

The heavy feeling immediately swallowed me and I took one step back, cautiously scanning the room from the door. I knew someone lived in there. I hesitated, but then decided to go on into the room and try to pretend that nothing was wrong. I quickened my steps as I opened one of the large stalls and hung the strap to my bag up on the hook at the top of the door. I casually unzipped the bag and pulled out my workout clothes. Still, I could not shake the feeling that someone was watching me. I changed my clothes as modestly as possible and I felt a little silly. Then, I came out and met James in the equipment room.

"Somebody's in there," I said as I stepped onto the treadmill.

"Oh, geez! Not again. Do you find ghosts everywhere you go?"

I paused as I decided how I would answer his sarcastic question. "Sometimes. I can't help it that this place is loaded. I'm telling you somebody is there watching. I almost could not stay in there."

We finished our workout and, once again, I had to go into that restroom. It still gave me the shivers and I hurried to get out of it again. The rules of the Senior Center required us to sign out when we left, so I went to the lobby to do so. Behind the counter, a woman sat reading a magazine.

"So, how was your workout?"

I knew this woman knew all the history of this building and the curiosity got the best of me. I looked at her and decided to ask about that bathroom.

"Has anyone ever told you that the Lady's Room is haunted?"

She set her magazine down and stood up to come closer to the counter. She gave me a very big smile.

"Oh, yes. Many times! You do know what that room used to be, don't you?"

"No, what was it?" This was bound to be good.

"This whole building used to be the Fort Hospital and that bathroom served as the surgical suite. Lots of people died there."

Well, that explained everything. There was not one ghost there, but many ghosts. I did not have to ask about the rest of the building because I could feel it, but she seemed to be waiting to tell me more.

"What about the rest of the building?"

"What do you think? Can't you feel it?"

I nodded and she smiled. She began to fill me in on all that she knew about the spirits in the building. She described all of the sightings very carefully as if discussing some of her friends, and she told me several stories of things she had gone through during her duties there over the years.

One particular story really made me laugh. It seems that the local high school had asked for permission to have a Halloween Haunted House in the building. With permission granted, the students had very eagerly set up every possible way to scare little kids in the different rooms, mostly upstairs. Halloween came and the special effects began all over the building. Little kids were running around screaming everywhere. This went on for several hours and the Haunted House was a huge financial success for the students.

The students left the building as soon as the event ended, leaving her to tidy up and close everything down for the night. She had very carefully gone around closing all of the windows and turning off all the lights. Just as she opened the door to exit for the night, she turned back to look into the building.

Suddenly, every window and every door in the building opened and closed violently at the same time. Her husband saw it from where he was waiting in the car in front of the building. She just stopped and held onto the front door.

"Okay....we won't ever do it again!" she said. The door she was holding onto violently pushed her out as it slammed shut. She told me was never the same again at work.

Another incident I experienced there at the Fort involved a woman ghost. Being new to the community, I had not heard the reports concerning the old restaurant building I was supposed to help decorate for the Junior Prom. I knew that I did not like going upstairs there because I could feel something.

I walked into the restroom upstairs to decide if we needed to include decorations for that room. Instantly, I felt watched and so sad. What is it about bathrooms anyway? When I came back out of the room, I must have had a funny look on my face because one of my students asked me what was wrong.

"I don't know....I just don't like that room."

She smiled and said, "It must be the White Lady."

"The what?"

"You don't know about the White Lady?"

"No. What about the White Lady?"

She began to tell me all about the legend. Supposedly, a woman was engaged to a soldier there at the Fort. She planned her wedding eagerly for when the soldier returned back to the Fort and her reception was to be held upstairs at this restaurant. The problem was that her fiancé found a new love where he was stationed and married her instead. The White Lady's sadness drove her to throw herself off the balcony of the building and she has been seen all over Fort Clark Springs ever since.

I absolutely could not force myself to go back into that restroom. The sadness was so very overwhelming that I avoided it completely. At other times, an icy feeling passed through me as I innocently stood watching the Prom. I never felt comfortable in that restaurant.

I soon learned that spirits can be attached to material objects. I am sure that I do not fully understand how or why this happens. Maybe these objects are things that were special to the deceased person in some way. It makes sense if you think about it. Ghosts are attached to houses, so why not to other things that were special to them in life?

The first time I experienced this occurred when I had gone to an antique dealer with my mother-in-law. I did not go there to buy anything, but I looked around the building while my mother-in-law made a deal with the owner for some canisters.

I rounded a corner and found the most delightful antique vanity. I had always wanted a special place to sit and apply my makeup in the morning. It seemed like my husband always needed to shower just at the same time I was getting my makeup done. The steam condensed on the mirror and I could not see anything. So, this vanity looked really great. The oak needed work, but the six drawers would hold everything I needed. It only had one problem. I felt a spirit staring at me from the mirror. I could not even look at the mirror in the fear that I might see something there besides myself.

Still, I really liked the vanity and had looked everywhere to find one like it before. I decided that I would not let a spirit stop me from buying it. Finally, I looked defiantly into the mirror. A feeling of anger and sadness filled me almost immediately. It was as if someone had spent many hours staring into this mirror in great distress. The feeling was a combination of anger, disappointment and depression. The joy of finding a long-sought vanity finally overcame my concern over the feeling in the mirror. I decided that I would find a way to deal with it and even asked God to help me with it.

I paid the dealer and my husband loaded it onto the back of the truck. God answered my prayer. The vanity bounced in the back of the truck and, as we hit a rock on the dirt road to my house, the mirror broke. When we got to the house and I saw the broken mirror, I was actually relieved to see it. I went to a glass shop and got it replaced and never felt anything bad emanating from the vanity again.

Another incident occurred when my husband attended a meeting in Bastrop, Texas. I drove him to his meeting and took off happily to explore the famed shopping in the little town. The first store I came to was an antique store.

I walked into the store and the owners greeted me.

"Good morning! Is there anything in particular that you are looking for?"

"No, thank you. I am just looking."

"Great! Just to let you know, there are three floors to our store. Just go down the stairs to the other floors."

"Thanks!"

I walked all over the first floor and found several interesting items. Then, I decided to try the next level down. I walked down the stairs and as I did, I felt company. I was not alone there even though there were no other customers or workers there. I hesitated halfway down the stairs as I felt that. Then, I decided to go on down anyway. Several of the items had spirits attached to them. I actually got the chills when I walked up to them. The feeling was especially strong when I approached a section of dolls.

Dolls have every excuse for being haunted. Think about it. Young, tenderhearted girls give them strong love and carry them around with them. The emotional investment is huge. I was not especially afraid of these feelings, but I knew I did not want to take one home with me. I decided to go to the next level of the store.

As I descended the stairs, I knew immediately that the number of spirits on this level was huge. There were not just a few ghosts here. They were having a ghost party! I gulped and kept going down the stairs. As soon as I got to the bottom of the staircase, I felt completely surrounded. I could hardly breathe. And these were not friendly spirits. I turned immediately and practically ran up the stairs. I stood at the top of the staircase and stared down into the lower level and I knew something was staring back at me. I would not be shopping on that floor of the store.

Several years later, I found a large secondhand store and decided to look around. When I walked in the door, the owner greeted me. So did something else. I tried to act like nothing was wrong as I walked around the store. I felt like there were many attachments there, but one particular corner just exuded the presence of a spirit. I could almost make out the form of a man who ducked behind a rack of clothes as I came around the corner. I think he could feel that I knew he was there.

About that time, the owner came to me and asked me if she could help me find anything in particular.

"No, but I do have a question for you."

"Okay."

"Do you have strange things happening here in this room?"

Her expression changed radically.

"Yes! How did you know?"

"I can feel it. You have something here that is attached to an item."

"Yes, well, it is a very expensive something. We close down the building at night and turn off all the lights and air conditioner. When we get back the next morning, all the lights are on and the air conditioner is running full blast. The electricity bill is huge!"

"It's over in that corner right now. It looks like a shadow and I believe it is a man."

"To be honest, we are selling out because of him and his high electric bills. I just can't afford to run this store anymore. I don't know how to get rid of him."

I felt bad for the woman but I did not feel free to try to get this ghost to move on. I never heard from God that I was supposed to do that. I know that I can get into some pretty bad trouble if I start doing things like that without express instruction from God. I bought a walking stick and left the building knowing that the ghost would stay. The couple has since sold the building and a church has moved in. I have to wonder if they have strange things going on in there or if the spirit left with whatever object to which it was attached. I have not gathered the courage to ask the people who attend the church."

INSPIRATION

Life in the city eventually drove us out to live on a ranch just outside of our small, West Texas town. A wonderful path wound around the perimeter of the ranch and I walked on it daily. I told everyone that this walking was exercise, but what it really accomplished for me was an escape from my teenagers and all their raging hormones.
I always started my walks with prayer as I felt so close to God out there. He listened as I poured out my soul to Him about everything in my life. The walk always lasted an hour, but the prayer often did not. As I continued my trek around the ranch, my mind began to wander and I began to form a plot for a book.
Each day, the plot flowed into my brain and I wrote it down immediately upon getting back to the house. Before I knew it, I had written a book. I wrote it as fiction, but I based it on facts that I found in the news. We published *Weapon of Jihad* in 1999.
http://www.amazon.com/Weapon-Jihad-revised-biowarfare-

ebook/dp/B00507U10C/ref=sr_1_1?ie=UTF8&qid=1361298814&sr=8-1&keywords=weapon+of+jihad

The book centered on a plot by Iran to attack the United States with a nationwide epidemic of Smallpox to weaken the country, and then follow with an actual military attack out of Mexico. We did not know at the time that some of the story we wrote would become history on 9/11. Many things we included in the plot happened. Later, when people asked how we knew these things before they happened, we realized that the plot had come to me immediately after prayer.

I wrote that the enemy would use our own planes against us. I wrote that there would be Islamic terrorists easily crossing into our nation through the border with Mexico. I wrote that the terrorists waited quietly for their cues to attack. I also made a completely fictional government for Iran and Iraq, long before Saddam was removed. I wrote that Saddam would be removed. In my book, Iraq becomes a puppet government of Iran and they form a coalition to attack our nation. As I write this, that relationship between those two nations appears to be forming. We will soon be pulling our troops out of Iraq and Iran has definite plans of taking over in Iraq, at least in powerful influence. All of this was written two years before 9/11.

I sent the book to every possible member of Congress and government organization in an attempt to keep it from actually happening. Of course, the book never became a bestseller; we sold only 500 copies, but I believe that I was supposed to get the message out as a warning. At least we now have enough Smallpox vaccine to protect our nation's citizens against this terrible disease. However, the rest of the story can still happen because all of the vaccine is in Atlanta. There is only a four-day window between exposure and vaccination if a person wishes to avoid the disease. We all know from the recent H1N1 flu vaccine fiasco that it would be impossible to vaccinate the nation in four days if all of the vaccine stays in Atlanta. The epidemic would go through the nation like a wildfire and all that vaccine would be useless, that is, if the enemy did not manage to blow it all up.

    I still occasionally send a copy of the book to someone I feel may have some influence on vaccine distribution. Still, so far, nobody is listening.

HELP FROM GRAMS

As the children grew up, we very busily chased the three teenagers to their various sports and activities. I had several different worries about different members of my family at this time. I was only getting about five hours of sleep each night, so I did not let worry stop me from sleeping. Apparently, Grams was paying attention to my little situation.

We gave our Grandmother the name Grams because it seemed to suit her personality. She lived to be one hundred years old before she died, and she lived with a spunky attitude that fit the red color of her hair when she was young. She stood six feet tall and her fire-engine red hair warned everyone not to mess with her.

Grams had been gone about a year and a half when I started hearing odd footsteps upstairs in our two-story house. It sounded like somebody was pacing back and forth up there when nobody else was home. I heard it so clearly one night when James was gone that I got out of bed and took my pistol upstairs to investigate it because I was certain somebody had broken into the house. After going through all of the bedrooms and closets carefully, I realized that nobody was there. Still, what was I hearing?

I asked James if he had heard any of it and he just shrugged his shoulders and shook his head. Even if he had heard anything, I am sure that he would not have confessed it. I began to think that maybe he was right. I was hearing things. That is....until my daughter heard it too.

She had come for a visit and we sat on the couch enjoying a little catching up. I had mentioned to her on the phone several weeks earlier about the footsteps and she had basically ignored me. But now, she kept looking around and finally stopped me in the middle of my sentence.

"Do you hear that?"

"What?" By then I had learned to ignore the sounds.

"Those aren't footsteps. That is stomping!"

"Oh, yeah. Happens all the time," I said and casually continued the conversation. The fact that she heard it too helped me to know that I was not losing my mind, but I had decided that whatever it was did not represent a danger.

Then, the footsteps began to cross my bedroom at night. The wooden floor creaked with each step as it crossed from the door to my dresser. At first, I thought that it was my husband walking around, but I found him asleep in the living room. Night after night, the footsteps crossed my room. It woke me up and I would sit up and look in their direction to find nothing. It began to irritate me because it interrupted my sleep.

Finally, one night the footsteps continued until about three in the morning. I sat up over and over and found nobody. Determined to get to sleep, I turned over and put my pillow over my head so I would not hear them. But, somebody would not be ignored that night.

I had cleaned out my purse on my dresser and left a pile of receipts sitting under a paper weight. I planned to deal with them the next day. I was forced to use the paper weight because I sleep with a fan blowing in the room.

I still heard the creaking of the footsteps. Suddenly, I was pelted with receipts. I threw the pillow off my head and looked over to my dresser where the receipts had been stored. The paper weight had moved off of the receipts and over about a foot away from where I had left it. I sat up and began to talk to the air.

"What?!! What do you want? Stop it! I'm trying to sleep!" I said loudly. I was angry now, but I had to go to the bathroom. After taking care of business and getting a drink of water in the bathroom, I walked back towards the bed. Then, I heard footsteps going from the dresser and leading out of my room to the hall. I decided to follow them.

I followed them down to the hall to the living room where I found that a family member had left the computer turned on. There, on the screen, was a manuscript of a chat session. It turned out to be a very enlightening chat session. I learned that night that one of my family members really needed my intervention. I cannot imagine what would have happened with this family member if I had not been made aware of the true situation.

The next week, I spent a lot of time with that family member and the problem was resolved. Later,

I realized that somebody had taken the effort to wake me up and take me to the computer to read the chat. Somehow, I felt like it was Grams. She always was a take charge person. I never heard the footsteps again and I am happy to say that my family member is fine today. I believe that Grams helped me in that situation.

THE NEXT GENERATION

One of my favorite parts of the gift has been my connectivity with my children and grandchildren. Since we are spread across the state of Texas by many miles in different directions, it is nice to know that I can read the important things in the lives of my family members as they happen.

This is nothing unusual in that most people will tell you that they will have a "feeling" about their family members and it turns out that some emergency or event has occurred. My mother and her mother were famous for calling their children and asking, "Is everything okay?" Many people have this ability and even confess it readily.

My gift takes it a little further. My grandchildren show themselves to me in dreams long before they are born. Sometimes this happens before the mother even knows they are pregnant.

My first grandchild, Kimberley, and I carried on long and exhaustive conversations when her mother was pregnant with her. I went to sleep with high expectations of visiting with her. She completely fascinated me. Each night, I dreamed that I was sitting next to her. The strange part of this dream was that she presented herself as a fetus but spoke to me like an adult. We discussed everything. I remember one particular night when her hair began to come in.

"Oh, look! Your hair is coming in."
"Yes, it is."
"I see that it is going to be very dark. I bet it will be beautiful."
"You think so? I hope so."

And so it would go every night. I was able to remember what we had talked about when I awoke and daily filled James in on what I knew. By the time she was born, we were best friends and we still are best friends. We can spend hours on the phone. But, those nightly discussions were only the beginning of our connectivity.

When Kimberley reached the age of two, she began to have ear infections. By this time, she lived in another city with her mother so I did not have daily contact with her. Still, we stayed connected somehow. My ear would start hurting and there was no reason for it to do so. I did not have a cold or any sinus problems, but my ear would start hurting so bad I wanted to cry. I even went to the doctor and he told me there was nothing wrong with my ear. The next day, my daughter called me and told me that Kimberley had an ear infection. Oh-h-h. It did not take long for me to put this together. When Kimberley had an ear infection, my ear hurt. I finally knew that, if my ear hurt, I should call my daughter.

"Hey, check Kimberley's left ear. She's got an infection."

"Right, Mom," my daughter would say. Then, she would take Kimberley to the doctor and be told that she had an ear infection. I was very happy when Kimberley outgrew her ear infections. Those things hurt both of us.

This connectivity proved to be a two-way connectivity. Kimberley knew when I was distressed. Being a two-year-old made it difficult to express, but she did her best.

I remember one particular day in the spring when storm clouds gathered at my ranch. I walked outside to get a good look at them and saw several small dips coming out of the clouds as they churned. Suddenly, a pencil-thin line dropped out of the sky and landed just beyond the barn. I freaked out and went running back into the house just in time to hear the phone ringing. I picked up the phone and heard Kimberley's two-year-old voice.

"It's okay, Grandma."

"Kimberley? What?"

"It's okay, Grandma."

Then my daughter took the phone.

"Sorry, Mom. Kimberley speed-dialed you. I don't know what's going on with her but she was freaking out."

It seems that my daughter had been doing laundry and was in the process of transferring the clothes from the washer to the dryer. Kimberley came running in screaming.

"Call Grandma! Call Grandma now!"

"Okay. We'll call her as soon as I finish putting this load into the dryer."

"No! Now! Now!" she yelled as she ran back out to the living room where she found her mother's phone. She pushed the number that she knew was mine from earlier calls her mother had helped her make. She just knew that I was scared and had to tell me that it would be alright. Amazing. She has my gift.

This revelation made me very happy, but it also made me feel concerned for her. I knew how I had grown up not understanding what was happening to me, and thinking that I was strange somehow. To be surrounded by people who do not believe anything you tell them is not funny. I knew that it all would be so real for her, but not to her parents. This sounded so familiar.

I decided that I must teach her all I knew about the gift so she would not spend her youth wondering about her sanity. As soon as she got old enough to understand, I began to explain it all to her. She would tell me when she felt something in her room and I would help her deal with it and discuss the whole process with her so she could battle these things on her own. I made sure she knew God and Christ and grounded her in faith. She would tell me about something she feared.

"Kimberley, who lives in your heart?"
"Jesus."
"That's right and He is bigger and stronger than anything you fear. He went down into Hell and defeated the enemy. They must obey Him and they fear Him. So, do not fear....fight! His angels surround you. You have nothing to fear."

I taught her how to pray for God to send His angels to protect her. At every opportunity, I stressed to her the power of God. Once, as we drove toward

Houston, three different tornadoes dropped out of the clouds. She panicked when she saw them.

"Grandma! Watch out! Don't drive into it!"

"Let's pray against it. Pray with me. Dear God, please keep us safe as we travel and cause that tornado to lift back up to the clouds. Clear it from our path. Thank-you, Jesus, for hearing our prayer."

The tornado lifted up and she squealed with delight. Before too long, the second one dipped down.

"Grandma! Look! Another one!"

"Okay...what are we supposed to do now?"

"Uh...pray against it?"

"Right!"

So we prayed against it again and, once again, it lifted back up into the clouds. Still a third tornado popped up again and, as if to reinforce the lesson, we prayed against it and it disappeared. The whole four-hour trip proved to be one big prayer lesson. When we got to Houston, my daughter asked Kimberley what we did for the whole trip.

"Grandma taught me how to make tornados go away!"

My daughter looked at me. I shrugged.

"When Grandma babysits, there will be a price."

"So I see."

She knows that I teach Kimberley as much as I can every time I get together with her. She let me take her with us to Corpus Christi one year and I decided to take her to go see the Lexington. My plan really did not include any ghost training. I simply thought she would enjoy the history lesson. But, when we got onto the Lexington, we realized that it was extremely haunted.

She feels the presence of ghosts just a little differently from me. She actually gets a shiver down her spine. I just feel them. So, we walked all over the Lexington and periodically we both stopped dead in our tracks. She would shiver and look over to me. I knew exactly what she meant and I would just nod to her.

"Where do you think it is?" she would ask. I would point and she would agree with me. We had a great time and are hoping to go there again. I did not know that the Lexington was supposed to be so haunted until I saw an episode of *Ghost Hunters* featuring the ship many months later.

I watch her as she goes through some of the very same quandaries I experienced at a young age. She badly wants to share her experiences with her friends, but I have cautioned her about that. We have discussed the fact that not everyone has these experiences and that others might be a little frightened of things they do not understand. People do not understand things that they have not experienced themselves. I have told her all of the social problems I ran into on my journey through life with this gift. Hopefully, she will not have to suffer the same mistakes I made.

A very important part of our discussions involves the fact that our gift is a gift from God. I have made sure that she understands that she must always use the gift for the glory of God, not herself. She also now understands that the enemy would love to hijack the gift to use against God. I have tried to caution her about how to avoid those tricks of the enemy.

TIFFANI AND BROOKE

When my second granddaughter was born, I wondered if she would be like Kimberley. I never had any conversations with her before she was born, but I knew that may have been because of some of the special circumstances that surrounded her mother when she was pregnant.

My daughter-in-law is a beautiful person who was raised by a loving family. Being the first-born in her family, she helped to raise her two siblings. Her mother, Olga, lived a Christian life and did her best to be the mother they needed.

Of course, when Jessica became pregnant, it meant that the baby would be the first grandchild for her family. Olga stepped into the role of grandma with great gusto and eagerly anticipated the birth. Her eyes sparkled when she spoke of her coming grandbaby and it was all she thought about. She laughed and enjoyed all of the process of putting on baby showers and baby shopping. But one day, I had a horrible feeling and I knew I had to call my son, Josh. I was driving down a highway when I made the call.

"Josh? Is everything okay?"
"Are you calling because of what happened?"
"Uh....what happened?"
"You haven't heard?"
"No. I've been in Uvalde. What happened?"

I listened and choked back tears as he described the horrible car accident that had happened only twenty minutes before. Olga was a passenger in a car that got shoved forward into traffic on a busy highway by another driver who did not stop behind them at the stop sign. Olga was quickly transported to San Antonio, but she never regained consciousness and died only a few moments after they got her to that hospital. Jessica was seven months pregnant with Tiffani.

Poor Jessica had just lost her mother right before the birth of her first baby. I felt so bad for her and I worried about them as I watched her sob in anguish. She barely had time to begin to see past the pain when Tiffani was born.

Tiffani came into the world, surrounded by all of us... and Olga. I felt her presence in the room and I hugged her loved ones.

"I just wish Olga could have been here to see her," one of them sobbed as I held her.

"She is here and she is very happy," came out of my mouth.

Olga stayed with Tiffani and I often felt her presence when I went to visit my son. We did not know just how much she stayed with them until Tiffani was old enough to talk. When she turned three, Tiffani began to spend time playing in her room, talking the whole time. Jessica heard her talking and finally decided to see who she was talking to. She stepped into Tiffani's room.

"Who are you talking to?"

"Olga."

That reply made Jessica stop and think. Tiffani had never met Olga and Olga only spoke in Spanish. Tiffani does not know Spanish. Jessica had made sure that Tiffani knew who Olga was by telling her all about her other grandma, so Tiffani was comfortable with her.

"But Tiffani, Olga only speaks in Spanish. You don't know Spanish. How can you talk to Olga?"

"I don't know. I understand her though."

Jessica decided to play along.

"So, what does Olga say?"

"She says that you do not have to take the flowers to the grave anymore because she is not there. She is here."

This statement out of the mouth of a three-year-old floored Jessica. When she told me about it, I told her it did not surprise me. I knew Olga had been there when Tiffani was born and it made complete sense to me that Olga would do her best to visit Tiffani since she had been anticipating playing with her so much. Jessica relaxed about it and soon became quite used to hearing Tiffani visit with Olga. She liked the idea that her mother was in her home, though she did not understand it.

When Tiffani turned six, something happened to the beloved relationship. One day, as Jessica drove with Tiffani strapped into her booster seat, Tiffani started sobbing inconsolably.

"What's wrong Tiffani?" she asked.

"I can't talk to Olga anymore."

"What do you mean?"

"I can't see her anymore. She stopped coming to visit me," she sobbed. She just could not understand.

Jessica told me about it and we discussed what that meant. I told her that many times children can see spiritual things much more clearly than we can and they lose this ability as they grow older. It does not mean that the spirit is not there. It simply means that the child has lost the innocence required to see them. I still believe that Tiffani is gifted and I still believe that Olga is there with her. I tried to comfort her the next time I saw her.

"Tiffani, Grandma Olga is still with you and will always be there. She is watching over you even if you cannot see her or hear her. Maybe, another day, she will show herself to you again. But know that she is there and that she loves you dearly. I can still feel her here and I think if you stop and close your eyes, you will feel her also."

She seemed to understand what I told her and she smiled at the thought. I am quite sure that she will exhibit more of the gift as she matures. Even now, she has dreams that are unexplainable. I try to keep in touch with where she is with the gift so I can explain as much to her as I can. I think it helps her just to know she is not alone and has some guidance.

A few years after Tiffani was born, my daughter gave birth to another daughter, Brooke. Brooke has shown many faces of the gift, much to the chagrin of her mother. She has told her mother of a man that is in her room who talks to her. I have gone to her room and prayed for angels to protect Brooke from any evil. The man stopped appearing but her dreams are powerful and I believe she will later exhibit more of the gift.

DERRICK

My only grandson, Derrick, came into the world a year after Brooke. His circumstance was also special in that he had a twin that died early in the pregnancy. I am curious to see what comes out of that relationship with his twin. I know that we all have souls, even as fetuses, so I know he was probably close with his twin at least for a few months. I know he is able to see and visit with spirits because of something that happened one time while we stayed in a condo up on the mountains.

The minute I walked into this condo, I knew it was populated. I tried not to say anything, but I kept my eyes open for anything unusual happening there. I was later able to "see" three different spirits when they actually introduced themselves to me one night when I got up to go to the bathroom. The group of spirits was interesting. One lady sported an outfit much like a saloon girl. Another spirit wore a gray beard and mustache and his hat looked like something that old miners used to wear. The last spirit was a man with a mean expression on his face.

I sleepily acknowledged their presence and asked nicely that they would behave around my grandchildren. The next day, my daughter-in-laws confessed to me that they felt something in the condo so I told them what I knew. We all agreed that it seemed harmless.

The next day, one of my daughter-in-laws told me that she had heard Derrick talking to someone in one of the rooms. She walked in and found only Derrick.

"Who are you talking to, Derrick?"

"Johnny," he answered casually.

"Who's Johnny?"

"He lives here and he has a funny hat." He went on to describe the old miner I had seen earlier.

"Oh. Okay."

But the spirits kept their agreement with me and kept their interference to a minimum. But it did show me that Derrick is also gifted. This has become readily apparent as he has grown a little older.

When he turned four, he began to talk to someone in his home that nobody else could see. His parents quizzed him. "Who are you talking to, Derrick?"

"My friend."

Derrick's friend became a constant presence and Derrick happily played with him for hours every day. Derrick asked his friend questions and then waited for an answer. We all thought it was really cute that he had an invisible friend. But I must confess that I wondered if it might very well be an actual spirit. But all the joking stopped one day when Derrick made an announcement.

"My friend is really my twin brother." He said it in a very matter-of-fact manner but it had an immediate effect on his mother. Derrick had never been told anything about the twin with whom he had shared his mother's womb. In fact, his parents and all who knew him had been careful never to mention it when he was around.

So, his mother quizzed him. "How do you know?"

"He told me."

"Oh." His mother just stared at him and then looked around the room. "Is he here now?"

"Yes."

"What does he look like?"

"He looks exactly like me."

"Oh."

So Derrick began to stand in front of a mirror to have discussions with his twin. He thought nothing of it, even though it freaked the rest of us out completely. That certainly confirmed what I was feeling anyway.

Then one day he made another announcement. "I have given my twin a name. His name is Jayden." So his conversations with Jayden continue, even though he is now six.

But I know that Jayden is real now. Not only can I feel him around when the family gathers, but he makes himself known in other ways. This Christmas, Derrick and his sister got remote-controlled helicopters. Derrick and I were in the living room and the rest of the family was dressing for the day at the back of the house. Derrick played with his helicopter and then put his remote down on the table in front of me right next to the remote for his sister's helicopter. Suddenly, his helicopter took off flying into the living room. Derrick yelled, "No Jayden, no!" Even with all my experiences, I had never seen anything like that. Jayden was playing with the helicopter. After a few seconds of flying around the room with nobody holding the remote, the helicopter landed back onto the table in front of us. As I sat there with my mouth hanging open, Derrick just continued along like nothing had happened.

So, Derrick not only has my gift, he far surpasses it! I watch him in amazement. But I know that a day may come when he no longer sees him. Or, he may just continue to see him despite growing older. I will be there to help him either way. It will be very interesting to watch him grow and learn. I am even thinking that he may have things to teach me.

MIRANDA, AUBREY, NAOMI

Miranda, my fifth grandchild, showed herself to me before she was born also. I saw her as a toddler riding on a toy horse. At this point, I will describe some of the confusion I feel when I see the grandchildren before they are born. I often cannot tell what sex they will be, especially if I see them as a toddler. I get no understanding of their gender. I only see what I see. I made the mistake of saying that I thought the child was a boy because of the short hair I saw. She turned out to be very much a girl; it just took a while for her hair to grow longer. On her first birthday, I saw her as I had seen her in my dream. She sat on a toy rolling horse exactly as she had been shown to me. She is a very strong person and I am watching her eagerly to learn about her gift.

Last year, I began to have dreams of a little girl. I had no gender confusion this time because she obviously had very long hair. In the dream, she would take my hand.

"Come on, Grandma, let's go."

So, I knew she had to be a grandchild. She came to me many times and she led me all around as she held my hand. Now all I had to do was find out which of my children was expecting. It did not take long. While we were on a family vacation, my daughter-in-law revealed that they were working on another baby. She was disappointed that she had not become pregnant yet and asked me to pray. We held hands and all prayed together asking God to send us a baby.

"Yeah!! Now we're going to have a baby!" little Tiffani sang as she danced in a circle.

She was correct. Nine months later, Aubrey was born. As she lay in the bassinet at the hospital, I took her little hand and wrapped her fingers around my little finger.

"Come on, Aubrey, let's go," I said. She smiled at me. I know that people say that babies do not smile at that age, but she definitely smiled at me when I said that. It was her way of acknowledging that she was happy I had gotten her messages. I feel very close to her and I am quite sure that her gift will be strong. She is now two and going through the usual two-year-old tantrums. But, even in the middle of a huge tantrum, she will stop immediately if I reach out my hand to her and say, "Come on, Aubrey, let's go."

A few months ago, I saw another vision concerning a grandchild. I saw my other daughter-in-law with her two-year-old daughter and another baby. I kept seeing this so I gave her a call to see if she would volunteer anything to me.

"Oh, I was waiting to see if you would call. I am late with my period and I feel pregnant, but I am still on birth control."

"Oh, you are already pregnant and that baby is very cute!"

Naomi's birth confirmed everything I had seen. Once again, I was unable to tell my daughter-in-law what the sex would be because of the short hair, but the description I gave her of Naomi's hair line and face shape were accurate. These two characteristics are different on her sister's face. I was able to tell her that she is carrying this baby very low, which the obstetrician confirmed later. She is one now and I am excited to see how the gift will manifest in her.

Recently, I had another dream concerning the grandchildren. My daughter-in-law who was pregnant with Naomi at the time stood with me and she held a baby girl. Lying on a table next to me was a baby boy. I talked to my daughter-in-law.

"I'm supposed to take care of this baby, but the parents did not leave me any diapers or bottles. What am I going to do when he wakes up hungry?"

Then, I realized that the baby boy was wide awake and apparently did not need anything. He just lay there smiling and cooing. He did not need a bottle or any diapers. When I woke up, I knew that this was a baby boy who was waiting in the wings somewhere. That explained why he did not need anything yet. The fact that I was supposed to watch him in the dream told me that I am just supposed to pray for him until it is time for him to come join us in our family. I asked all the women in the family and they all told me that they were not pregnant, but I know that I will know this grandson someday.

FINDER

Another aspect of my gift presented itself shortly after this time. It came as quite a surprise to me as it appeared. Once again, words that I had not thought blurted out of my mouth.

My husband thrives on chaos. He must. He never puts anything away and is constantly losing important things, like keys. Every time he would misplace his keys, he would start tearing up the house looking for them. I would do just about anything to find them before he emptied every drawer and messed up all my stacks.

One day, the key finding fiasco began again. I started turning everything over, helping him look because he was in a big hurry. Suddenly, words came out of my mouth.

"Oh, stop it! They're in the trash."

I stopped in my tracks. I knew I had not thought that thought. Why would they be in the trash? They had never been there before so it was not experience speaking.

"Hmm. Why not?" I audibly asked myself as I headed to the trash can.

He had heard me say it too, so he began to go toward the trash can also.

"Why? Did you throw them in the trash?"

"No. I don't know why I said that. It just came out of my mouth."

"Right. Okay, if I dig through this trash and they're not there, I'm going to be mad."

He opened the lid and pulled out the bag. There, at the bottom of the bag, something heavy rested in the middle. He put his hand out to touch it and it jingled like keys. Then, he reached through the trash and pulled them out.

"How did you know that?"

I just shook my head. "I don't know. I just knew."

He gave me a strange look and took off out the door. I sat and thought about that for a few seconds. It was a new one for me and I really did not understand it.

"That was weird," I said to myself.

It was not long before this new gift showed up more frequently. Each time, someone would be frantically trying to find something. Each time, I just knew where it was. Sometimes, I actually saw it sitting in its hiding place. It was, however, not something I could do on call. Believe me, I wished I could just do that whenever I wanted, but it did not work like that. Apparently, someone else had control over it and it only happened when it was very important. I tried several times to find things like earrings I had lost, but to no avail. God was in control.

One particular incident occurred when my daughter was getting ready to move from an apartment to a house with her husband. I had promised to go down to help take care of Kimberley and I did not get there until the day before the move. I arrived to find my daughter and her husband frantically searching for something.

"Where is it?" my daughter complained.

"I gave it to you last. If you don't know where it is, I sure don't," my son-in-law answered as they turned over cushions on the couch.

"What are you looking for?" I asked as I finished hugging Kimberley.

"Oh, just the key to the storage compartment. The furniture that would not fit in this apartment is stored there and the movers are coming in the morning. They're supposed to pick it up and take it to the house with all this stuff, but tomorrow's Sunday and the storage place is closed so we can't get another key. I had it a while ago." My daughter continued to open drawers in the kitchen as she searched.

Suddenly, I saw it. It hid in one of the boxes they had already packed. The box it was in sat at the bottom of a stack of boxes in the living room. Without even hesitating I shared this information with my daughter.

"It's in that box in this corner of the box," I said as I pointed to the box.

My daughter just stopped and stared at me.

"What? Why would it be in there?" she asked. "I packed those this morning and I know I had it since then."

"I don't know how, but that's where it is. I am just sure."

She gave me a look. "How do you know?"

"I saw it there."

"Uh huh...I see." She turned away and kept flipping things over in her search.

I sat down on the couch and watched them and I had to wonder why they would not even try to look there. They were looking everywhere else. It was so plain to me. That was where it was and I knew it. I began to get frustrated with them. A few minutes later, I tried again.

"Um...it's in that box in that corner of the box."

They just ignored me and kept on going. It was as if I had not said anything. Nobody even reacted to me this time. I let them search and decided not to bother them anymore. If they were not going to listen, they deserved to keep searching. Finally, they sat down and gave up.

"Maybe we can call them tomorrow and get a hold of somebody to let us in," my daughter suggested.

I tried one more time. "It's in that box in that corner of the box."

My daughter stood up angrily. "Okay, Mom. I'll show you it's not in there just to make you stop saying that."

She walked over to the stack of boxes and lifted each one down until she got to the bottom box. Then she ripped off the packing tape and opened the box. I could not help myself.

"It's in that corner."

She glared at me and reached her hand into the box in the right corner. Her fingers closed in on a pair of cut-off shorts and she pulled them out.

"Are you happy now? Does this look like a key?"

As she waved the shorts in the air, the key fell out of the pocket. Her mouth fell open and she just stared at the key on the floor for a few seconds. She looked at me and then at her husband.

"Did you see that? Did you see that?" Then she walked out the door and stayed for a while. When she came back in, she looked at me in wonder.

"How did you do that?"

"I don't know. I just saw it."

Most of the time, the finder gift involved personal items or things belong to a family member. Sometimes, however, it happened when other people needed it. One particular incidence of this occurred when I was teaching one day.

My student rode her horse often and she had fallen off and hurt her eye. She bravely came to class anyway and did her best to not miss any school. Her doctor gave her some eye drops for pain and as long as she used them, she was able to perform in class just fine. She came to my class in the afternoon right after lunch each day. One day, she came in and put her head down on her desk instead of working like the other students. This was not characteristic for her so I assumed something was wrong. I walked up to her desk and leaned down.

"What's wrong?" I whispered so the other students would not hear.

"My eye really hurts."

"What about your eye drops? Did they stop working?"

"No. I lost them," she answered, almost crying. Immediately, I saw where they were.

Now, usually, I kept my little gifts to myself and my family. I definitely knew that nobody else would understand them so I just never mentioned them. My students often wondered how I knew where they were hiding when they skipped class. I was known to walk out of class and go straight to their hiding places. I never explained how I did this. I let it be a little piece of teacher mystique. It was always good to keep the students guessing.

But this time my student was in pain. I knew I could help her find her eye drops, but it would be impossible to do without revealing my finder gift. I watched her frown in pain and knew I had to help her, regardless of what it revealed. I leaned down and whispered in her ear.

"Your eye drops are on the ground in the grass where you got out of your mother's car at lunch."

"Really?"
"Go get them."
"Now?"
"Yes, now."

She looked at me, and then looked around at her classmates. By then, curiosity caused some of the nearby students to look up and watch us. She put on her coat and went out the door. I went back up to the front of the classroom like nothing happened. Still, the other students kept looking at each other with questioning looks until my injured student walked back into the room. She seemed to understand that I did not want to announce any of this to the others, so she slipped quietly into her seat, smiling. I walked back to her desk.

"Well, did you find it?" I whispered.

"Yes. It was exactly where you said it was. How did you know?"

"I don't know. I just did."

She gave me a puzzled look but then she smiled. Her pain was gone. Nobody asked about it until a few days later. My student had finally told her friends what had happened and they were amazed. One by one, other students came into my room.

"Can I ask you a question?"

"Sure."

"I heard that you could find things and I lost a pair of diamond earrings last week that my Dad gave me. Do you know where they are?"

I had hoped that it would not come to this. I saw nothing that would tell me where the earrings were and I knew I did not control this gift. I waited a few seconds longer hoping I might see where they were. Nothing happened.

"Uh, no. Sorry. It is really not up to me. God decides what I see and He has not shown me anything about the earrings. Sorry."

Her disappointment showed but she understood what I was telling her. Still, other students came in one at a time for a few weeks wanting the same kind of help. I was able to help one of them find her laptop but the rest were out of luck. When we had a few extra minutes, they would ask me about it and I told them what they wanted to know, hoping that they would realize that it was the power of God working through me. They seemed to understand.

A NEW GIFT

The gift then morphed into something else. When people went missing, I would see where they were. The first time this happened, it startled me and scared me. I would see things that were happening to people as they died and immediately after they died. I do not understand this very well.

It feels to me like I am being shown these things by the spirit of the missing and dead person. It is almost like they want me to help find them. Many of these visions are still a mystery to me, but others have resolved to be exactly what I have seen.

One example of this was a case involving one of my mother's friends. She had travelled to Dallas from San Antonio to visit friends and then left to go home at the end of the weekend. She never got home and everyone was searching for her, hoping that she was not harmed. The second my mother told me about her, I saw what had happened.

She was driving home and she drove off the road to the right of a bridge, plunging into a creek. I saw her car halfway submerged with only the tail end out of the water. She died in the driver's seat and she was still there. A sound came with this vision. It was the sound you make with the letters sc or sk. I did not see the letters but I only heard the sound. I understood that the name of the creek had that sound in it. She wanted to be found.

It really bothered me. It was like that scene in 'Close Encounters of the Third Kind' where the man is driven to build a model of a mountain out of mashed potatoes and rocks. I was driven to find that creek. I opened a map of Texas and began to search along her route, looking for creeks beginning with that sound. The closest one I could find was Schooler Creek. I did not know it but I had forgotten that the sound was somewhere in the creek name, not necessarily at the beginning. When they found her, the scene was exactly as I had painted it only it was in Bosque Creek. Apparently, I forgot that sq could also make that sound.

This brings up something that is still a mystery to me. So many times, I see everything correctly, but I manage to mess it up in the translation. After the facts of the situation are revealed, I have this moment of "Well, of course!" and do not know how I missed it. Apparently, one little mistake can make the whole vision useless. Still, there has to be a reason that God shows me these things. It is written in the Bible that we see through a looking glass dimly. In my case, it is very dimly sometimes. It causes me to hesitate and wonder what I am supposed to do with it.

When the television series 'Medium' started I was immediately hooked. There was a woman who saw things and dreamed things that she did not understand. Many times, she messed it up, but many times she got it right. I related to her and was quite relieved to know that there were others out there like me. I watched as she suffered through great frustrations with this gift.

The difference between her situation and mine was that she had a relationship with a District Attorney who believed her. I get these visions, but I have no outlet. What am I supposed to do with this stuff? Am I supposed to do anything at all? Maybe I am just supposed to pray. I pray every time, but sometimes that is all that is accomplished. It may very well be that prayer is all I am supposed to do in certain situations. I have learned to be patient. God will do with my gift whatever He pleases and I do not have to understand.

When the congressional aide, Chandra Levy, disappeared, I saw her lying where she had been murdered immediately after I heard the report on the news. She lay surrounded by greenery and shrubs with a white flower. There was a drainage pipe nearby and the whole place was dark and in the shade of tall trees. I saw the path she had taken to get there. A rock fence meandered down a hill and into the trees where she lay.

When I saw that, I did not have a clue as to what to do with it. It bothered me because I knew she wanted to be found. Later, she showed me a face. The man's face was thin and very light-colored. He had very dark hair and he was somewhat nice looking. I saw him as he smiled in her direction.

In the days during the investigation, reporters followed the Congressman suspected of her murder. One of the scenes shown on the news report showed him walking to a microphone, followed by his entourage of aides. He did not look like the face I saw, but one of his aides did. The aide appeared to be distraught as he stood behind the congressman. It was clear that he must have had feelings for Chandra.

The frustrating part of all of this was that I could not help. I even resorted to calling the 800 number for information on the crime. The woman who answered the phone clearly sounded like she thought she was dealing with a crazy person. She courteously thanked me, but I knew my information would go no further. My name is now probably on some government list of crazies. It was all so clear to me that I knew I could walk her path exactly if I could just get there. I knew I could take them right to her.

Later, the news announced that they were very sure that she had been buried under a newly poured parking lot. When they said this, I reacted with complete disbelief.

"No way...she's in the woods," I yelled to my husband when I heard it.

My husband did not know what to do for me. On one hand, he knows I can find things because I do it for him all the time. On the other hand, he cannot understand how I could possibly know anything about this case. After all, I am not there or even close. He really does not believe in spirits at all and I had confessed to him that it was Chandra's spirit giving me the information.

Later, when they found her body, they showed the location where she had been found. It was exactly as I had described. This did not surprise me, but it did surprise my family who had been forced to suffer through my visions. I still do not understand the connection between the young man I saw and Chandra. The man they accused of her murder did not look like him at all. All I can guess is that maybe he was the last person to talk to her before she met her murderer. I clearly saw him talk to her and look at her lovingly. A few weeks ago, the case made national news again. Officials are thinking of releasing the man they convicted of the crime due to lack of evidence. The man's cell mate, who had stated during the trial that the defendant had confessed the crime to him, has recanted his testimony. So, the case has not been solved. I feel like it may involve the dark-haired man I saw but I cannot be sure. Like I said, I do not have a handle on this gift.

Natalie Holloway disappeared in Aruba and the whole process began again. Natalie desperately wants to be found. She showed me what happened and where they hid her body. I will try to tell you exactly what I saw as much of my error seems to be in my interpretation.

I saw the accused young man looking at me. I am assuming that it was not me, of course, but Natalie. Something happened and Van der Sloot reacted in fear. His eyes got big and he moved my face back and forth. Then, he looked all around in what seemed to be a panic. The next vision involved the hiding of her body. They (yes, he had help) carried her over to the water's edge and stuffed her into something metallic. It is a metallic structure just barely big enough for her body. It has some kind of damage that looks like something had been blown out of it as in an explosion. The edges of the blown-out area are rather sharp and about a foot and a half in diameter. They stuffed her into this structure so she would not float to the top of the water.

Now, I will try to explain what I think happened, though I have learned that this part may be partially wrong. Interpretation is often where I err, but here it is. Van der Sloot drugged Natalie in order to have sex with her. Something went wrong. Maybe it was an allergic reaction to the drug or maybe he gave her too much. Anyway, it killed her. When it did, he panicked. He could not take her to a hospital or to the authorities without having to explain his crime so he decided to hide it. He got his friend to help him take her to the metallic structure that they knew from previously swimming in the area. They put her in there and concocted a story, which they successfully maintained for a while, but now has changed several times.

After the government initially declared Van der Sloot not to be a suspect, Natalie's mother put real pressure on them and they once again opened the case. The news showed video of the authorities out close to the beach, digging for evidence once again. I watched this in great frustration because I knew somehow that they were so close to where she rested. I yelled out at the TV.

"No! Go to the left and down the cliff!"

I knew that they were only a few hundred feet away. Once again, if I could have gone there, I could have walked straight to the site of her burial. I still know that I would be able to find her if I could just go to Aruba. Even better, the officials could find her if they would just listen to me.

I gave the information I knew to a website link in an article about Natalie. Apparently, the information was never acted on. I also wrote to Natalie's mother to tell her where her daughter was buried. She either ignored it or never got it. Natalie has given me a message for her mother. She has seen the great suffering her mother has gone through.

"Tell her that I am so sorry for putting her through all of this. I should have listened to her. I love her so much."

I did send that message to her mother, but I am quite sure that it was never received. I audibly told Natalie that I was sorry I had failed her. I tried everything I knew to do. Somehow, I knew she smiled when Van der Sloot was arrested for the murder of his second victim. Maybe he will finally give her family some closure by disclosing Natalie's location now that there is no hope for his freedom. I pray for that.

Visions came to me for other people declared missing on the news. Immediately after hearing the news report, I heard the words "too late" on some of them. The days following always proved that the person was indeed dead. Sadly, little Caylee was one of those. I read her mother over the television and knew she had killed her daughter. I did, however, pray for her grandparents.

One case involved a woman who had disappeared and all of her friends were frantically searching for her. I did not hear that it was too late so I decided that she must still be alive. I had no overwhelming urge to pray for her safety either. Later, authorities found her hiding in California. She had run away and was never in any danger. But, most of the time, I hear that it is too late. When I hear those words, I pray for the family and that they will have closure. I am not always shown where the body is hidden. This is just as well because I never know what to do with that information.

Sometimes, a spirit comes to me for help and there has not been a report on the news. One such spirit showed me a vision of her body floating in a slowly moving river overgrown with foliage. As she floated, she quizzed me.

"Why did he murder me?"

It really bothered me because she seemed so sad. The man she loved had murdered her and she could not understand it. I prayed for her to have peace and go home to God. The news report came a few days later. Authorities had found her body in the foliage of a river and they arrested her husband. They showed a picture of her and it matched what I had seen. Her husband had been having an affair and also wanted to collect her life insurance. I felt so bad for her. She was an innocent victim clueless as to her husband's evil ways.

Others have come to me and I still have not figured out who they are. One such murder victim showed me what she was seeing from where her body was buried in a shallow grave. She showed me that she was behind an old, torn down building in a quiet part of town. She neglected to mention what town. She did tell me her name was Melissa and that she had gone out on a date with the man who killed her. I may never know who or where she is. I prayed for her and apologized to her about not fully understanding. I did search missing persons for people named Melissa with no success. If I ever see that building, I will know it and go look for her. I do not know what else to do. Unfortunately, this happens too often.

A TEXAS THANKSGIVING

    Beautiful Oak trees graced the path as we walked in the warm Texas sun. Crisp puffs of wind refreshed the air. The Thanksgiving Dinner had just been amply accomplished and the dishes were washed, so we decided to take a walk.

    The path we traveled meandered easily through the ranch that belonged to my in-laws. My granddaughter, Kimberley, walked along beside me, telling me all about everything in her life and watching for wildlife in the brush. Our noisy footsteps in the fallen leaves jumped a cottontail rabbit and it scrambled toward the dry creek bed. We laughed and kept on going toward the other house on the ranch.

    Our goal was to make it to the other house, which stood approximately one mile away from my in-laws' house, and then turn around and go back. That should shake down the pecan pie and maybe make room for the pumpkin pie. We made it to the house and went inside to get a drink of water. We sat on the couch resting and drinking the water as we continued our conversation.

"Your grandfather and I are going to be moving to this house in about a year," I told her.

"Really? You're gonna live here?"

"That's right...and we will be closer to you then so you can come see me more often."

"Wow! Are you going to get some horses?" She loves horses so much that her room is filled with every kind of horse model and bedding.

"Probably. Then you can come and ride." She smiled and leaned back on the leather couch.

BANG, BANG, BANG, BANG! We nearly fell off the couch as the sound of somebody hitting tin outside the house startled us. We looked at each other and stood up and it continued. The intense clanging filled the air and hurt our ears with each hit.

"What was that?!" I screamed as we ran to the windows and looked out. "I think some of your cousins must have followed us."

We frantically skidded through the house, searching in all directions as we reached each window. We saw nothing unusual except a frightened jack rabbit frozen in place and staring in the direction of the sound.

"They must be hiding," I said. "Let's go see."

Afraid of what I might see, I slowly opened the creaking door just enough to see out. I looked in every direction and held onto the door with one hand and Kimberley with the other. She fought to get past me and see out the door. I looked back at her and put my finger up to my lips to tell her to be quiet. She nodded so I opened the door a little more. I held her hand and we haltingly stepped in the direction of the obnoxious sound, which had stopped by now. Going past the rose bushes and scanning carefully in all directions, we rounded the corner of the little house. The pile of tin came into view and we stopped. Nobody was there. Looking in every direction, we stood there searching for any movement. If the cousins were hiding, they were doing a really great job of it. Kimberley looked up at me and I shrugged.

"Well, what was it?" Kimberley asked.

I looked at her and shook my head. "I don't know. But you heard it too, right?"

"Uh-huh," she nodded.

The crisp grass crunched as we walked back toward the door of the house. Suddenly, we heard them. The sound of playing children filled the air. Squeals and calling preceded the peals of laughter and giggling. We stopped in our tracks and looked at each other again in surprise. The sounds floated from a nearby area of thick oak trees and brush.

"Grandma, is there a house over there?"

I scratched my head. "No, I don't think so."

"So, what is that? Are there some kids in there?"

I frowned. "I don't think so. Why would there be kids there? I know there is not a house anywhere over in that direction."

"But Grandma, you can hear them can't you?"

"Hmm. Maybe there is a house I don't know about around here somewhere. When we get back to Granny Mary's house, I'll look at the map of the place. If there is a house with kids, maybe you can play with them when you come see me here."

We walked towards the sounds of the children, expecting to walk up on a house in that direction. But, instead of getting louder, the sounds began to fade as we approached the tree line. Then, they were completely silent.

"OK, that was strange," I said as we turned back to the house.

We sat on the couch and drank our water before we left to return to Granny Mary's house. The path led past an old, run-down house abandoned on the ranch decades ago. The old cedar planks wore peeled layers of white paint. Parts of the front walls had fallen down, so the old red bricks of the fireplace could be seen still supporting part of the falling roof. The missing walls also exposed gaping holes in the floor boards of the front room. A doorway past the living room revealed chipped, faded linoleum and rough cabinet doors sagging on only one hinge. Mason jars perched on some of the dusty shelves and an old tin cup sat on the warped countertop.

As we approached the house and we stepped onto an oak-covered path, an eerie feeling came over me as if someone was watching me. I could almost see someone out of the corner of my eye standing on the cracked foundation at the edge of the house, leaning on the door frame. Suspenders held his old-fashioned brown pants up and the sleeves of his white shirt were rolled up. He wore an old, brown hat. The look in his eyes was menacing and his mouth held a slight smirk. I looked away toward Kimberley to see if she had noticed him and when I turned back to look at him again, the man had disappeared. I said nothing to Kimberley so she would not be frightened. That was all she needed after what we had just been through. Suddenly, she stopped.

"Oooh, Grandma, somebody's watching us!" she said as she visibly shivered.

"Yeah, I know. Let's just keep going."

Our steps quickened and we said nothing as we hurried down the path. We finally reached Granny Mary's house, went inside and demanded to know who had followed us down to the house. Everybody was sitting or sleeping on the chairs and couches in front of the big football game.

"I don't know, Kimberley," was all I could say. The ranch map showed no nearby houses.

About an hour later, my daughter-in-law and I went into the dining room to visit. We sat there and talked about the day and began to make plans for the Christmas gathering.

"Where did you go a while ago?" she asked.

"We went down to the other house."

I began to tell her what had happened. She just looked at me like I was crazy. She did not keep that look on her face for very long.

Suddenly, the freezer door on the refrigerator across the room opened. We looked at it, and then at each other. It made no sense. We were the only people in the room. Well, we could not let it stay open, so we both stood up to go close it. In response, it slammed itself shut! Something had followed us back. Our mouths fell open and we went running into the living room to tell the others what had just happened. Nobody believed us....except Kimberley.

My husband and I moved into the house across the ranch a year later. The Thanksgiving events proved to be only the first episode of a story that continues even today. Kimberley loves to come and walk through Terabithia with me. We refer to our favorite place on the ranch as Terabithia because it looks much like the place that the movie with that name was filmed. It is a place of beauty, inhabited by the spirits of laughing children where I go to meditate, relax and think. I have very carefully kept Kimberley updated on all the events here at the house as she asks about it every time we talk. Our shared difference has made us close.

MOVE INTO A HAUNTED HOUSE?

When we retired, we decided to finally move to Mary's ranch. My father-in-law had died suddenly and left my seventy-eight year old mother-in-law trying to run the ranch. Of course, she could not do it on her own. So, we packed up all of our things and moved into another house already on the property, the one my granddaughter and I visited in the last chapter, where we heard children laughing and banging on tin pots near the house.

I had told all of my friends about all the events involving the house and they all thought I was crazy to move into it. I really did not fear it for some reason. But, as we began to move our furniture into the house, I began to wonder if they were right.

The first thing I noticed was the face in my bedroom. The little ranch house had not been lived in for about three years. Apparently, a tree had grown too close to the house and a branch had rubbed a tiny hole in the tin roof just over our bedroom. A little rain added to this to create a small leak that had stained the ceiling. The only problem was that the water stain looked just like a grimacing face.

I stood under the water stain staring at it. The outlined head included a set of eyes with huge dark circles under them. It also sported a nose and a mouth with an evil grin. On the top of the head on the right side, a dark stain looked like a bleeding head injury. Hmmm.

"James, come here and look at this."

"What?" he quizzed as he came around the corner into the room. He saw me staring at the ceiling. "Yes, I know. I'll fix it."

"No, that is not what I am talking about. It's a face.... a very evil looking face."

"Oh, no...not that stuff again." He knew that I was sure the house was haunted.

"No, just look at it. It has evil eyes, a nose, ears and an evil grin. It also has some kind of injury on the top of its head."

"Oh, gee, Karen, give it a rest! It's just a stain. You're one of those people who can see bunnies in the clouds, that's all."

"You mean you can't see it? Look at it. It's plain as it can be."

The problem was that the face was located right over where my head would be when we slept in the room. Well, if it did not bother him, he could sleep under it.

"Well, then. You can sleep on this side of the bed."

"Oh, no...that is your side of the bed," was all he could say as he left the room.

I thought about it and decided he might be right. It was just a water stain. Maybe I was being too sensitive. And I believed this until my four-year-old granddaughter, Tiffani, walked into my room a few days later.

"Oh, Grandma. You have a monster over your bed!" she said when she saw the face.

A few weeks later, the whole family came to visit and a houseful of screaming grandchildren ran through the house at high speed for the entire weekend. I think that may have scared out anything that was too scary there. Still, every night before I go to sleep, I pray for God's angels to do spiritual warfare around us and keep us safe as we sleep there. That is the only way I will ever sleep under that face.

Two years after we moved into the house, I learned the identity of the man at the old house. A group of elderly women sat at the Dairy Queen visiting and I joined them to wait for my car to be serviced next door.

"Where do you live?"

I described how to get to our house.

"Oh, that's the old Gatlin house. I know all about that place. My grandmother used to buy chickens from that man that had a house there. He was mean. He lived there before the two houses were built. The Gatlins bought the place from him and then built the houses there."

"What do you mean?"

"Oh, he used to chase all the women and he got into fights with their husbands all the time. He was also mean to his kids. He got killed when a branch fell on his head."

Oh my goodness! That explained the wound on the top of the stain monster's head. Was it simply coincidence that I had a water stain that looked exactly like the builder of the old house? I do not think so. I think it was more like ghost art.

It seems to me that mean-spirited people might not want to move on after they die for obvious reasons. They are afraid of where they will be going because they know they have been bad in life. It is like they would rather hang around somewhere in between life and eternity to avoid hell. That may explain why so many ghosts tend to try to bother the living. Their meanness transfers with them in death and they still like to torture innocent victims.

I also believe that our God is much more forgiving than we can understand. Any God who will send His only Son to die for us sinners is serious about giving us a chance to spend eternity with Him. I cannot fathom that such a God would turn away a spirit if it confesses its sins and asks forgiveness, even if it has already passed. This is my belief even though I know most people do not agree.

So, this in mind, I walked back to the old house one day to address the mean spirit there. I spoke to the air.

"I heard all about you the other day. I know that you were mean while you were alive, and I know why you do not want to go home. But, I am not here to beat up on you. I think maybe I can help you."

I explained all about my belief that God would still forgive his sins if he confessed and asked forgiveness.

"I know you cannot be happy here, watching everything you built fall apart and being so lonely. You need to try to go home. I am not trying to make you leave. But I know you would be much happier if you could be with your loved ones. I will go now and you can think about what I said. I hope you can find happiness."

I do not know if he listened to me but I have not felt his presence since that time. I sincerely hope he was able to be forgiven and go home. Or, he may have decided that he did not want to hear what I had to say again, so he is hiding from me. At any rate, he has not bothered us since.

TERABITHIA

Two chapters ago, near the end of A Texas Thanksgiving, I mentioned that my granddaughter and I heard the voices of children playing close to the house I later occupied. This episode is an ongoing story of discovery about this place.

The voices of the children sounded like they came from behind our house in a heavily wooded area. I walked back there one day just to see what I could find. The trees are huge and they gracefully fall over and cover a path through the area. A feeling of peace surrounds you as you enter these woods. I immediately fell in love with it and I named it Terabithia because it reminded me of the woods in the movie of the same name.

A strange thing happens when you walk down that path. Serenity envelops you and even the wind stops blowing. This caught my interest. The wind blew ferociously outside the area. It stopped completely when I walked into Terabithia. I paused, confused. I turned and walked back out to find the wind still blowing. I would understand this if

Terabithia was in a valley, but it is not. I love it. Sometimes I go there to write or just to think.

During this time, I went through some surgery that kept me under anesthesia for about seven hours. The procedure was supposed to be a thirty-minute procedure and I was supposed to go home when it was finished. I went in at eleven o'clock in the morning and came out at six o'clock as the sun was coming down. It really confused me as I came out of the anesthesia and found myself being wheeled down a hospital hallway on the way to a room where I would stay for four days. But, that was not the only thing confusing me.

Two children held onto the gurney and rode along as we went from the day surgery unit to my room. A little girl with blond, wavy hair rested close to my shoulder and a little boy with dark curls and suspenders rode behind her. The little boy looked all around and asked a question to the little girl.

"Why are we here?"

"Shhh. We have to help her now. She is our voice."

This totally confused me. I looked over to my husband who was walking along beside the gurney.

"Who are those two children?"

"What two children?"

"The children hanging onto the bed...who are they?"

He exchanged a funny glance with the orderly pushing the gurney.

"Karen, there aren't any children hanging onto the bed."

"Yes there are. You can't see them?"

I do not remember anything else until later that night. The two children had disappeared. I did not see them again but I thought about them a lot. I was quite sure that these were the children that we had heard at Thanksgiving but their conversation mystified me. I did not understand all of this until later.

A few weeks later, I went to choir practice and returned home after darkness had fallen. As I turned down the lane to my house, I noticed a light in Terabithia. Actually, it looked like a window with a light in it. I stopped driving and stared at it. I knew there was not a house there. What was I seeing? The window stood exactly where the children's voices had led Kimberley and me. I got to the house and went inside the house to call James to come look at it, but by the time he came out, it was gone. I am sure he thought I was just going crazy again.

The next day, I walked over to Terabithia to try to figure it out. I stepped down the shaded path and reached the area where I had seen the window. There was nothing there. I never saw it again.

Several months later, my husband hired a man to do some bulldozing on the ranch. I very carefully insisted that Terabithia must be left alone. I could not stand the thought of the destruction of such a beautiful place. James assured me that he had discussed this with the man running the bulldozer.

A few days later, I heard the dozer nearing Terabithia. I raced out of the house and caught the dozer entering the edge of Terabithia. I frantically waved my arms at the man operating the machine to stop him. He could not hear me so he turned the machine off. The poor man did not know what hit him.

"What are you doing?!!!"

"Your husband told me to doze this area."

"What?!!! NO, NO, NO! Not in here! Go back out! Leave this alone!!!"

The poor man just looked at me like I was a crazed woman.

"No really! Go back out of here!"

He ducked his head as he stepped back onto the dozer, shaking his head. He started up the machine and drove it out of Terabithia. I stood there with my hands on my hips staring at him as he left. Then I turned to walk slowly to the center of the area. I spoke to the air.

"That was too close. Don't worry. I will not let him doze in here."

I had to chase him out two more times before he finally gave up. He later apologized to my husband about not accomplishing the Terabithia portion of the ranch. He told James that I just kept chasing him out and that James would have to talk to me about it. I stood firm about it and Terabithia did not get dozed. I did not understand until much later what had driven me to be so rude to that poor man. It was the children.

The children had their own way of keeping people out of Terabithia. I noticed that every time I walked into it, I suddenly became aware that I was in real need of a bathroom. I went running off to the house as fast as I could go. I thought it was just me, but I noticed that it happened to everyone I took into Terabithia. I mentioned it to each person after it had affected them and we would go get another victim to try it out on. It happened every time.

I began to think about it and I decided that it must be some kind of defense mechanism. If you did not want someone to stay in your area, what better way could you use than to send them for a quick trip to the bathroom? Finally, I spoke to the air when I walked in.

"Hey, could you skip the part where you send me running to the bathroom? You know I am not going to hurt you. Just let me come in."

I never had to go running out again. But, it still hits everyone else who enters. Later, I found out that it had even affected the dozer operator. It was a very good defense.

But, why did the children want to keep everyone out? I found out one day as I ambled through Terabithia after several months of rain. Terabithia was particularly beautiful at this time because of all the lush greenery. Moss covered all the rocky areas and rocks that I had never noticed before became obvious in their green jackets. Suddenly, I noticed two piles of large rocks. I went to investigate them and found that the piles were child sized and they had small headstones at the top of them. Nothing was written on the head stones, but they stood where the head of a grave would be. I had found the graves of the children. That is why they guarded Terabithia. It is their resting place.

I came to understand more about the day I first heard their giggles. The children were afraid of the spirit of the man in the old house and they were worried that he would hurt Kimberley and me. When we responded to his pounding of the tin by walking toward the old house, they called to us with their laughter so that we would be led away from him.

As I stood there looking at the graves, I had a vision about how they had died. The children had drowned in a flashflood in the dry creek bed a very long time ago. I have since learned that a huge flash flood killed many people in our area in 1936. I went to try to find their obituaries at the library, but there is a seven year time span there for which all the obituaries have been lost. I had to wonder why they were still here. It bothers me a lot to think about children lost and not able to go home to God.

I have heard that sometimes, children fail to go home when they die suddenly. It is like they are confused about what happened to them and that confusion keeps them earthbound. It bothered me so much that I finally went over to their graves and had a long talk with them. I tried to explain to them that they had died and what that meant. I told them about Jesus and that He was their friend and He could be trusted. I told them that it was alright for them to go with Him home to God where they would find their parents and I encouraged them to be brave. Sadly, I am quite sure that they did not go home. We still feel them there and they still send visitors to the restroom in a hurry.

I have also heard that more aggressive spirits are able to hold other more passive spirits, like those of children, earthbound. I have to wonder if the spirit of the man in the house has been holding the children there. The distance between my sighting of the man and the graves of the children is only a few hundred feet. Hopefully, the man at the house went on and that will allow the children to go eventually. I have not felt the presence of the man since I had my talk with him so maybe he went on, thus freeing the children. I only hope for peace for all of them.

THE CLOSEST NEIGHBORS

Before the man's spirit left, he was our closest neighbor. The old house sits behind and catty-corner to our present house. What I have noticed is that the neighbors come over to bother me every time my husband works in the area of that house. The original event with the tin banging happened shortly after my husband's brothers began dismantling the old house. They have since stopped the process, leaving most of the dilapidated house there. The next set of events happened when my husband was building fence in the area.

I waited until everyone left the house and I took the opportunity to wash the dishes. The cats finished their meal and took advantage of the fact that I was busy to jump up on the table. They knew I would not chase them off with my hands in the dish water. It was a daily routine. Suddenly, one of the chairs at the table just scooted itself back about a foot away from the table! The cats stared intently at the chair and I stood there waiting to see if it was finished moving. Satisfied that the show was over, I talked to the air.

"Well.....have a seat!" What else could I say? Then, I realized that my husband was working by the dilapidated house behind us so I added, "He's not going to touch the house....don't worry. He's only fixing the fence."

When my husband tore the tile off the bathroom in our house to remodel it, again, someone was not happy. That night, as we slept peacefully in our bed, the bedroom door slammed shut with force. I sat up in bed and stared at it. There was no wind in the house as the windows were all closed. In fact, I had placed a weight at the bottom of the door to hold it open so the cats would not be scratching to get in and out of the room. So, when it slammed, the weight had to have been moved out of the way.

"How did that happen?" I asked my husband who was rubbing his eyes and staring at the door.

I got out of bed and walked over to the door to open it. As I put my hands on the handle, I realized that it would not turn. I tried several times to turn it but it would not budge. Then, I tried to just push the door open. It refused to open. I tried again without any luck. It felt as if someone was holding onto the handle on the other side of the door and pushing against the door.

"James, it won't open."

"What?"

"It won't open...the door is stuck."

"What? Don't give me that. Do I have to get out of bed and go open it?"

"Well, look!" I yelled as I tugged and twisted and pushed on the door.

He got up and came to the door. He took the handle and turned it easily and pushed it open. I could not believe it! He gave me an irritated look and headed back to bed. I closed the door and tried it myself and the silly thing opened easily just like it had when James had opened it. The next day, I walked around the house audibly assuring whoever was there that we really were going to make it nice and no more stunts would be necessary. I never had any more trouble with that door.

I have since learned that I can prevent events by explaining ahead of time. For instance, when we remodel any part of the house, I walk around the house and tell the air all about it the day before the work starts.

"Okay, today we are retiling the bathroom. Don't worry, I promise it will look nice. He's not tearing it up."

My husband has told me that he plans to bulldoze the old house sometime soon. I am not looking forward to that because I know who will be picked on for that action. Further, he wants to put a small mobile home there to use as a guest house. I have a feeling that the mobile home will have all kinds of interesting things happening. Maybe I will have to write another book about that.

Still, periodically, fun things happen at my house. The latest episode took me by surprise as I have never heard of this type of contact. This takes a bit of explanation. Our home does not have central air and heat. We have window units where we can fit them. My bedroom, however, is very small and has closets along the walls so there is only one way to align our king-sized bed. The head of the bed rests along the windows, so we are not able to put a window unit there. Our only other option was to get a portable air conditioner for our room and it came with a remote. I keep the remote up on my dresser in one corner of the room and the unit itself is across the room in the other corner.

The air conditioner makes a ting noise every time you push any of the buttons. The remote allows me to change the temperature setting, turn the unit on or off and change the display from degrees Fahrenheit to Celsius. It also came to life one night.

As James and I lay sleeping, the air conditioner unit tinged and turned itself on. We did not need any air conditioning that night, so I got up and turned it back off. Then, it turned itself on again. It did this three different times that night, each time waking me up and requiring me to get up to turn it off. James declared that it must have a short of some kind and I bought that explanation...until the next day.

The next day, my son and his family came to visit us and I told my daughter-in-law about what had happened the night before as we walked into my room. The unit immediately dinged. We looked at each other and continued into the room.

"See? It's showing off for you," I said as we got into the room.

"Ding."

We looked at each other again. Hmmm. The unit stayed quiet for the rest of the day and my family left to go home. Then, the next day, it really started acting up.

I walked into my room and the unit greeted me.

"Ding, ding."

I stopped at my door and looked around. My cats were both resting on my bed, so it was not one of them walking on the remote. They were also staring at the remote, not the unit that was making all the noise. I looked all around the remote and decided to play along.

"Oh, hi....I see that you have figured out how to play with the remote."

"Ding, ding." Hmmm.

"Well, that's pretty talented."

"Ding, ding, ding, ding, ding."

"Really! It sounds like you could be quite musical with it."

"Ding, ding, ding, ding, ding...," it kept dinging for several seconds, each time using a different note. It was just like it was singing or playing an instrument.

"That was very nice."

"Ding, ding."

I could hardly believe it and it was almost too much even for me. This thing was communicating with me with that remote. I had never heard of such a thing before. I just left the room and went into the living room to think about that for a while. I had seen shows on the television that showed people using different devices to try to communicate with ghosts. Not one had thought of using a remote. I decided that maybe it was Mike or some other harmless spirit so I did not worry about it. That is until it took a bad turn.

I was preparing for bed one night a few days later and the TV was tuned to *Ghost Hunters*. The crew was using a thermometer unit to try to find cold spots that might indicate an entity. Suddenly, their thermometer started dropping from 72 degrees. It dropped all the way to 66.6. One of the men made a comment about the significance of that number. As if on cue, my air conditioner started dinging and the temperature was being changed. Down, down, down it dropped until it reached (yes, you guessed it) 66 degrees. I looked at this and realized that this was as close as it could get to 66.6 because the unit does not have a digit for tenths. My mouth dropped open and I reacted.

"Oh, so you think that's cute."

"Ding, ding."

"Well, it's not! If you are evil, I will not have you here. My Lord is Jesus Christ. I don't think your little 66 joke is funny. Now you change it back, or you leave!"

The unit dinged a few times as the temperature setting changed back to what it had been before.

"Thank you!"

"Ding, ding."

Then, I thought about it for a second. Maybe it was just trying to show off that it could do what the ghosts on the show could do.

"Okay. I understand that you might have been just showing off, but that kind of stuff is not allowed here. You can stay if you were just showing off, but you must not ever do that kind of thing again."

"Ding, ding."

That was the last I heard of the remote going off by itself for several months. Then, suddenly, the air conditioner sounded off again at five in the morning. I pulled out of my deep sleep.

"Oh, stop it!"

"Ding, ding, ding."

The pinging sound became almost frantic and began to sound like Mozart. It dinged like a small child trying to tell his parent something as fast as he could.

"Ughhh! Stop it!" I repeated. Then I got up and turned it off.

My husband decided that he had had enough fun and went to go get the coffee brewing. I got back into bed and slipped back into sleep. Within ten minutes the air conditioner turned itself on. I sat up and stared at it. Obviously, I was not going to be allowed to get any more sleep. So, I got up and walked over to turn it off.

I climbed back into bed in an attempt to try again.

"Ding, ding, ding, ding, ding, ding, ding, ding!"

The air conditioner was playing the notes like they were sixteenth notes. I sat up. That was enough!

"What?!!!! What do you want? You know I can't figure out what you are saying!"

I stopped for a second and then decided to call on God.

"God, is there something you are trying to tell me?"

"Ding, ding, ding."

"Uhhh, okay. Well I don't get it. But You do so I will just turn it over to You."

I began to pray, "My Father, please send your mightiest angels to attend to whatever this problem is that I am not able to understand. Protect and save anyone I am supposed to be praying for. Thank you, Father, for your help."

Periodically, the air conditioner sings to me still. James usually gets angry and leaves the room. Then, I pray the same prayer and it silences the noise. James is convinced that it is just a short. That may be true. I just have to wonder why it keeps on going until I pray and then suddenly stops. That is too much of a coincidence for me. I believe it is simply a way to call me to prayer. As to who is doing it, I may never know. I just respond.

EVERYWHERE I GO

My gift follows me everywhere I go. Sometimes this can be very entertaining. I find ghosts in many public places, especially hotels. I am sure I do not understand why ghosts hang out in hotels. Maybe it is because the hotel is a place the person enjoyed in life. Maybe it is where they died. To me, it is horrible to think that people died in the room or hotel I am renting. Still, I know it happens and the older the hotel gets, the more spirits it collects. Yet, I have found relatively new hotels that have unregistered guests. I will describe a few of the spirits I have found out in the public.

My sister and I traveled to Europe a few years ago. Most of the buildings we found had been built decades or centuries ago and had collected many spirits. Of course, the many castles are loaded with them. I remember one castle that unnerved me.

I had left the tour group going through because I needed to find a restroom. Coming out of the restroom, I found myself searching through the castle in an attempt to rejoin the group. As I walked briskly through the lower passageways, I came to a place that stopped me in my tracks. A very small room off to the left of the passage grabbed my attention and I stopped to cautiously look inside it. Something inside seemed to pull me into the room, but I could not stay very long. I shuddered as I felt completely surrounded by spirits in there and I ran out the door and back down toward the group. Later, I found the group and followed along as the guide explained the historical events of the castle.

The tour guide led us down to the same passage I had escaped from and right to the very room I had fled. There the guide described the horrible events that had occurred in that room. The victors of a battle had imprisoned two hundred men in that tiny room and did not know what to do with them. While they debated whether to kill them or keep them as prisoners, the men stayed in the tiny room without food or water for six months. They could not even sit down. The guide showed us the back of the room where a boulder appeared to be wet. She explained that it was called the 'Licking Stone' because it leaked an extremely small amount of water and the men would lick the rock in an attempt to survive. Eventually, all the men were slaughtered. I can tell you that they are still there.

We visited another family castle in Scotland. The tour guide gathered us all together in the dining hall and described the history of the site. Then, she told us that one of the upper bed chambers was haunted by a faithful servant who had been seen several times. She laughingly invited us to try to figure out which room it was and tell her after we explored the castle. I did not think about that very much. I was wrapped up in the whole culture of

Scotland and how the people lived in that castle. But, as I turned a corner into a room, I stopped short. I knew immediately that I was not alone in that room. And, I knew that there was more than one spirit there. When I got back down the winding stairs to the dining hall, I told the guide that the spirit she described was in the room with the green plaid bedcover.

"Why yes. That is the one. How did you know?"

"I felt him there and he is not alone." That little bit of news seemed to be something she had not been aware of before. I was not able to tell anything about who was in the room with him, but I definitely felt two different spirits there.

We then traveled to Iona at the very top of Scotland. There we found a beautiful church with a small chapel behind it. It is reported that this church was the first Christian church established in Europe and my sister and I walked around it in complete awe. As we entered the small chapel at the back of the main building, a surreal sensation surrounded us. I wanted to just stay there because it was so very peaceful. Then, we walked out of the chapel and around the building. As we walked, someone tried to introduce themselves to me. I was alone, yet I heard a voice.

"Gwyneth."

I turned and looked around me to see who had said that. Nobody was there.

"Gwyneth."

Okay. Apparently someone named Gwyneth wanted me to know her name.

"Hello, Gwyneth. Is this your home? It is truly beautiful!"

She must have been satisfied with my response because she stopped telling me her name. After researching the name and Iona together, the only Gwyneth I found was someone who is presently living. There is a Gwyneth who serves as an outreach person for the Church in Iona. Maybe I look like her or something. Or maybe there is a Gwyneth buried there. I guess this will remain a mystery for me.

A short time later, James and I traveled to San Francisco and stayed at a hotel there for two nights. I felt something strange about the room the minute we walked in, but I said nothing because James does not like to think about ghosts. I diligently tried to ignore the sounds of footsteps I heard walking around the room at night as we slept. I just played like I did not know anything was there. Apparently, the ghost was determined to get my attention.

James had used the little bottle of shampoo supplied by the hotel. It was half empty and resting on the far side of the bathtub in the bathroom. The morning we were going to leave, I went about the process of getting dressed and getting on my makeup. I stood looking in the mirror. Suddenly, the little bottle of shampoo picked itself up and threw itself across the room so that it hit the mirror and bounced back to the floor.

"Okay...yes...I know you're here but I do not want to deal with you. Leave me alone. We are leaving in a few minutes," I spoke to the air.

"What?" James asked from the other room.

"Oh nothing...just talking to myself."

Still another spirit introduced itself in a hotel room in Oklahoma City. I had driven there to attend a writer's conference and the trip took a full eight hours so I was tired.

I arrived at the hotel late in the afternoon, checked into the room and went down to some of the evening events of the conference. I met up with my friend, Pat, and some of her friends and we sat and had some drinks. One of her friends wore a T-shirt that said 'Oklahoma Paranormal Society.' I decided not to say anything about my experiences as I was, once again, in a situation where I was trying to make new friends. We all visited a while and then decided to turn in for the night to get ready for the next day's meetings.

I went up to my room and began to get ready for bed. I confess that I had that feeling, but I did my best to ignore it as I was alone and did not want to think about it. The room had two beds in it and I decided to sleep in the one toward the inner part of the room. I turned off the lights, crawled into bed and turned toward the wall, hoping to drift off to sleep. Just as I was going to sleep, I heard something behind me between the two beds. As I came out of my groggy state, I realized that there could be nobody there because I was alone in the room. I rose up on my elbow and looked back towards where I had heard the sound. I stared intently into the darkness and saw nothing. Suddenly, I heard a loud click and the lamp on the table between the two tables turned on.

I rolled over and sat up, staring at the light. I do not know what I was expecting to see, but there was nothing there. I stared at it for a long time. Okay, lights do not turn themselves on. Every hair on my body was standing straight up at the thought that I was that close to something I could not see. I took a deep breath and decided that maybe it was just a fluke. Maybe that light turned itself on all the time. Anyway, I was exhausted from driving all day and I decided to go back to sleep. I turned the light back off, laid down and rolled back over for another try.

It took a while to finally begin to drift off because I had been startled. Click. The light turned on again! Now I knew that someone was there with me. Further, I knew they were messing with me. Each time, the light turned on right when I was drifting to sleep. I rolled over and sat up, staring at the lamp.

"Okay...very funny! Now stop it! I'm tired and I need my sleep. Go bother somebody else!" I yelled into the air because I was angry.

The night passed without any further incident and I got up the next morning to go down to the conference. Before long, I saw the man I had met the night before who had been wearing the paranormal T-shirt. This time, I decided to confess to him the events of the night before. I told him what had happened and he looked at me.

"I'm sorry."

"You're sorry? Why?"

"Sometimes this happens. Something follows me home from a ghost hunt and then follows someone else more interesting later. We were at a hunt last weekend and I knew I had brought something home. Last night, I knew it was gone. It must have chosen to follow you."

I just looked at him.

"You're kidding, right?"

"No. It happens all the time."

"Great! Well, you might need to come get this one back. It made me get to sleep late."

I sat and visited with him about it and then confessed that I had always been a ghost magnet for some reason. He told me that some people just have that problem and invited me to go on the next hunt.

"Thanks, but I do not go looking for spirits. They come to me, apparently."

That night, I went back up to my room. This time, I spoke to the air in advance.

"Look. I have to drive home for eight hours tomorrow. Behave yourself and let me sleep. Thanks."

Nothing further happened and I left the conference with much to think about on the long drive home. I decided to go back to the conference the next year. I made sure I stayed in the same room where this occurred. Call it a curiosity. Was the spirit really one that had jumped to me from the ghost hunter, or was it a spirit that stayed in that room? As it turned out, nothing was waiting for me in the room so the investigator must have been correct. The spirit had jumped from him and followed me that year. I will go back again and stay in that room just to make sure.

Another incident occurred when I journeyed off to Las Vegas with my sister, Connie. We have been to Las Vegas many times before, but we had never experienced anything paranormal. We had no expectations that this trip would be any different. We arrived at the hotel and checked in, also receiving our keys to the room. This was the last normal event that occurred in that hotel.

We rode the elevator up to our room, which was on one of the top floors of the hotel. Connie slipped her room key into the key slot and it refused to open. She tried several times and each time, all three lights lit up. This indicated that someone was in the room and they had locked the dead bolt. We knocked and nobody answered. Then, I pulled out my key and the door opened without any problem.

We decided that she must have received a faulty key, so we put our totes in the room and went back down in the elevator to get another key for her.

"Is there a problem?" asked the woman at the counter.

"This room key will not work. The other one works just fine, but this one refused to open the door repeatedly," I answered.

"That's odd," she commented. Then, she produced another room key. "This should work better."

We laughed as we rode the elevator back up to our floor. We walked to the door and tried the new key. It did not work. Connie reinserted it several times and each time the three lights lit. I decided to try it myself so I took the key from her and inserted it into the slot. The door opened up without hesitation. We looked at each other in wonder. This needed some experimentation.

I handed my key to Connie to see if it would work for her like it did for me. The lock stayed locked. Then, I took my key back and tried it again. The door opened easily. Connie tried her new key and it did not work. I took her new key and the door opened. This made no sense at all.

"You must not have the touch," I commented as we entered the room to put away our things.

We spent the rest of the day out of the room and returned much later to get some sleep. Connie tried her key to see if it was some kind of time fluke but the door refused to open until I put her key into the slot. We laughed at the odd occurrence and went into the room to prepare for bed.

Connie managed to get to bed before I did by a few moments. I slipped into my bed a little later and closed my eyes to relax. Immediately, I saw the light. And it was a beautiful, flowing light in a color of blue that awed me. But, I knew what it meant.

"Connie," I said.

"Yes?"

"We are not alone in this room."

"Yes, I know. I just saw a black shadow drift across the ceiling."

"Great! That explains the lock."

"What do we do?"

"We tell it to leave us alone," I answered. I was tired and did not want to play.

"Okay. Go ahead."

"Okay, spirit, we know you are here, but you need to leave us alone tonight. We are tired and need our sleep. Behave!"

The ghost let us sleep, but began to play with us again the next morning. We went about the process of getting dressed as usual. Connie sat on a padded chair to apply her makeup. The chair had padded armrests and cushions. She set some of her items on the armrest, looked away and then noticed that the things she had put on the armrest had disappeared. She began to look all around to see if they had fallen off. She stood up and picked up the cushion to look under it. Then, she bent down to see if they had fallen under the chair. The makeup was nowhere to be found.

"Hey, Karen, come here."

"What?"

"I put my makeup on this armrest and now it's gone. I looked everywhere. Do you see it anywhere?"

I walked over to the chair and repeated the search process Connie had performed. I looked under the cushion and under the chair.

"I don't see it anywhere."

Then, I remembered that we had company in the room. And I remembered that Mike loved to play this hide-and-seek game with us. I turned to the center of the room and spoke to the air.

"Oh, Ha-ha. Very funny! Now give it back."

We turned around and found all of the makeup sitting on the armrest exactly where Connie had set it.

"Great....a prankster," I said.

"Yeah, great!"

The look on Connie's face showed her discomfort with the situation. She has been with me all our lives, but I know sometimes she does not believe me when I tell her things that happen around me. Actually, I was quite happy to have a witness this time, even though it was an unwilling witness. And this particular ghost was picking on her, not me.

We left the room and went down to the convention. A little while later, Connie decided that she needed to run up to the room. By the time she got to the room, she also needed a restroom. She fumbled with her room key and, of course, the lock refused to open. She stood there and tried over and over again. About that time, I arrived to hear her talking to the ghost. She must have been desperate.

"Come on! Let me in! I have to go to the bathroom!"

She tried her key again. It did not open.

"I'll show you my booty if you'll open the door!" she cried in desperation. The door opened.

"Great! Dirty old man ghost," I commented.

The next day, we got up and started getting ready for the day again. Connie kept a close eye on her makeup and it did not disappear this time. But, when she laid her bra down on the bed and turned around, it disappeared.

"Karen!"

"Yeah"

"Now he has my bra."

"See? It's a dirty old man ghost!"

I looked all over the room with Connie and the bra was nowhere to be found.

"Okay....very funny again! Give it back!"

The bra lay on the bed exactly where Connie had left it. We discussed all the possibilities. Maybe it was the spirit of some dirty old man who had come to Las Vegas and died there. Maybe his wife that he did not like looked a lot like Connie. Maybe he thought Connie was cute and just wanted her attention. But, we decided he was harmless and we began to have a good time with it. That morning, as we left the room, I spoke to the ghost as the door closed behind us.

"See you later, ghost."

As I turned to leave, I heard, "Bob."
I turned to Connie and said, "What?"
"I didn't say anything."
"I just heard somebody say, 'Bob'."

We looked at each other and smiled. I looked back at the door and said, "See you later, Bob."

We went down to the convention and came back later in the day. My key was buried at the bottom of my big purse. Once again, Connie's key refused to work.

"Come on, ghost. Let us in," I said. The door did not open.

"Come on, Bob. Let us in," I tried. The door opened. From then on, Connie's key worked as long as she acknowledged Bob's presence.

We found a booth at the convention that offered to take people on ghost tours. I stopped and visited with a man who was sitting there at the booth. I began to tell him that we did not need to go on a tour to find ghosts as we had one in our room. Before I could say anything else, the man, who apparently was clairvoyant, explained our situation to me.

"You have the spirit of a man named Bob who died of a heart attack in your room. He is enjoying your visit immensely and promises to behave from now on. He said he won't hide any more of your things."

I just stood there looking at him. How did he know all of that? Apparently, his gift was much stronger than mine. But, I was glad to hear that Bob had decided to be good. The rest of the stay went smoothly without any further pranks. The last night we stayed in that room, Bob decided to bring some of his friends to meet me. I lay down and closed my eyes. It was like a light show. Gorgeous intense colors flowed around me in many different shades. They did not frighten me and I rather enjoyed the show. I told them they were beautiful. There were apparently many ghosts in that hotel. As we closed the door for the last time in our visit, I turned and looked at the door.

"Good-bye, Bob. Thanks for everything!"

ANOTHER VEGAS TRIP

My mother had suffered with Multiple Sclerosis for many years. She had been diagnosed in a late stage of the disease, so treatment was not very effective for her. Still, being the spirited person she was, she did not let the disease get her down. Her positive attitude and love of travel kept her going for a long time.

One of the things she loved best was our annual trip to Las Vegas. My sister and I traveled with her and she loaded her scooter onto the plane and off we went. Every year, we stayed at Caesar's Palace where she practiced her role as the little old lady with the black glove. She wore the black glove because the coins she constantly won were very dirty.

She would drive her scooter up to a slot machine that she thought would do well, put in some money and begin to pull the handle. Almost every time, the machine would start to sing at her very touch. I did my best not to touch the machine because I knew that would stop her winning run. People stood in line behind her to jump on the machine because they thought it was the machine that was giving good luck. To their chagrin, the machine would stop singing the minute she left it.

The people at Caesar's knew my mother by name and they loved her. They paid for her room, meals and show tickets. Many times, they had to come out with IRS forms because she had won a very large amount. Needless to say, she greatly anticipated the trip each year.

A few years ago, the multiple sclerosis caused her to have major balance problems and she was forced to stop her yearly trips to Las Vegas. But, she had taught my sister and me well. We began to go to the Star Trek Convention in Las Vegas for our yearly sister trip, and we would always go to Caesar's Palace in her honor for one day. We would call her from there and tell her how much we missed her being with us. She carefully told us which machines to go to and I believe she traveled vicariously through us. We always brought back things to her that we knew she enjoyed. Every once in a while, she would mention that maybe she could escape one more time and go with us. We all knew, however, that it was impossible. But it showed that she still had the desire.

In June of 2011, I had a dream that woke me up wondering. In the dream, my front door opened and my grandmother walked in. Now, my grandmother has been gone since 2000. Needless to say, I got very excited in my dream and ran up to her.

"Grams! Wow! You look great! I have missed you so much!" And I excitedly rambled on until I realized that she was not even acknowledging me. So, I stopped and stared at her.

"What's wrong, Grams?"

She just turned and faced towards Cedar Park, looking expectantly away. My mother's nursing home was in Cedar Park and I knew it would not be long before I lost her.

When I awoke from the dream, I cried and told James about it. He assured me that it was just a dream. That was on a Thursday and I called my mother to be comforted by her voice. I decided it must have just been a nightmare because she sounded fine and that is what I wanted to believe.

The following Sunday, I received a call from my sister telling me that I had better get down to Cedar Park because Mom was dying and could go at any time. I hurried to the nursing home. I found Mom lying in her bed, mostly unresponsive. She would come out of it once in a while and look at us as we waited. We wondered what she was looking at because she kept talking to someone in the air.

For one whole day, she laughed and giggled and played with some baby boys.

"Oh, look! My boys! They're so cute!"

Now, my mother did not have any boys that lived. However, she had suffered through two miscarriages. One miscarriage occurred before I was born and it was a boy. Later, after she had given birth to my sister and me, she lost a set of twin boys. Apparently, she was playing with the sons she had lost and was having a blast doing it.

I want to mention this in particular because I know several people who have lost babies and they wonder if they will ever see them again. The answer is yes. I realized at that point that my sister and I had been the fortunate ones to be able to be raised by such a wonderful mother. We had gotten our time with her. Now, it was our brothers' turn to have her. I know now also that I will someday meet my three brothers. I am looking forward to it because I did not have any living brothers.

The next day, mother continued to decline. She kept looking up, smiling and saying, "Yes." Then, she would turn her head to the side and say, "No." She kept raising her arm up towards the ceiling and smiling. She was not paying any attention to us in her room. Her attention was totally intent on what she was seeing.

At one point, a doctor came into the room. "Is there anything I can do for you?"

"I want to know how to go up."

My sister and I just looked at each other because we knew what she was talking about. The doctor grew misty-eyed and answered, "You'll figure it out."

Later, I brushed her shoulder and asked her if I could help her any.

"I want to go up to the fan." She was talking about the ceiling fan. Once again, we knew what she was trying to do.

There was a bathroom in the corner of the room. At one point, I came out of the bathroom door and she turned to me.

"How did you do that?"

I exchanged glances with my sister. "Do what?"

"Get through the door."

I came closer to her and touched her shoulder once again. She turned and looked intently into my eyes and said, "You're very perceptive!" I did not know what she was talking about, but when I thought about it later I understood. She was mostly on the other side of the veil and when she looked at me, she saw what other spirits see when they see me. They can see that I can see them. This statement from my mother has clarified much to me. I understand better now why spirits seem to follow me around.

    I stayed with my mother all day and then my sister came to relieve me. I went home to get a few hours of sleep, but when I closed my eyes I saw a beautiful green spirit. It was very excited about something. I was not sure I knew who it was, but I knew by the excitement that Mom would probably pass soon. I could not go to sleep for a good while, but I finally drifted off to sleep. I only slept two hours when I was awakened by a call from my sister. Mom had passed.

    We gathered at the nursing home in Mom's room and wept together. Mom was finally free from her body that had kept her from living the way she wanted. We arranged for the funeral home to pick up her body and we headed home. I decided to go back to sleep as I had only slept for two hours, but the second I closed my eyes I knew that would not be possible. The green spirit I had seen earlier was back, now much calmer. And it had brought a friend this time. The new spirit glowed in a gorgeous purplish-pinkish hue and had sparkles within it. The iridescent edges rolled peacefully. I knew it was my mother, free to come see me at last. The green spirit, whom I believe was my grandfather, had brought her to me so I could know what she looked like and I could recognize her when she came to see me. I felt her happiness and relief. I started crying and laughing at the same time.

"Hello, Mom! You're beautiful!" Then I sobbed in relief for her for quite a while. I knew then that she could come see me any time she wanted to.

She has only appeared to me a few times since then. She showed me that she visited Dad's apartment, which made complete sense to me. I do not expect her to stay with me or even with Dad. It is hard to compete with Paradise! But I know she is watching over us.

A few weeks later, my sister and I went to Las Vegas for our yearly trip. We enjoyed ourselves and knew that, for the first time in a long time, Mom could come with us again. We went to Caesar's Palace and visited all of her favorite machines. Then we ate at her favorite restaurant and even ate the ice cream she so loved in her honor. We could feel her presence as we remembered her favorite places. I closed my eyes at one point and saw her there. I know she was smiling at us.

When we got home, I uploaded all the pictures from our trip to the computer. There, in the middle of one of my pictures, a huge orb stood beside me as I posed. I have always heard about orbs and I was not sure of what I believed about them. Now, I am convinced. My mother managed to get into our vacation pictures, confirming what we felt. I was tempted to label the picture with "me and my mother in Las Vegas."

Do not misunderstand me here. I miss her terribly. I realize that, even though I can see her with me sometimes, I can never just pick up the phone and talk to her again. Then again, I just talk to her without a phone! And, even though I can feel her presence, I can never hug her again. I guess I am still in a carnal state myself, because those physical things are still important to me.

Because of what I have recently been through, I understand the physical loss we must endure a little more now. I was always able to tell people who had lost loved ones that the separation was only physical. Our loved ones are able to be with us. I understand now that the loss of the ability to actually touch someone is painful. But, I am reminded that it is temporary. We will join our loved ones as spirits someday and that physical need to touch will be nonexistent.

DEATH CLOSE TO ME

As we grow older, so do our parents. As I mentioned in the previous chapter, sadly, my precious mother passed recently. It has been a very painful experience, of course, but the knowledge I have gained through my gift has softened it somewhat.

In the chapter Long Term Visions, I described a series of dreams I had over three nights. This happened 10 years before my mother passed over. I actually foresaw my mother's death in one of those dreams, but as it was a very cryptic dream filled with puzzling imagery, it took many years to understand. In fact, I still do not understand the complete meaning of the second dream.

To remind you, in the first dream, someone was asking me about water quality. In the second dream, I saw my own death, and the death of my mother who was riding a scooter, a symbol of the disability caused by the MS that eventually claimed her life, but after we died, we both stood up again. In the third dream, I saw an Army of tanks rushing across a desert to Israel with an unknown man leading the charge.

Eventually, after so much time passed with nothing related to any of the dreams actually coming to pass, I began to think that they were all just bad dreams. That is, until the first dream actually happened.

Ten years after the dream series, I found myself running a water testing lab. I had not really thought about the fact that I was doing that in my dream. I had taught for several years before I left to stay home with my children. Then, I opened the water lab, thinking that it would be a part-time job that would allow me more freedom to be a mother. The dream I'd once had about someone asking me about water quality never entered my mind as I opened that lab.

A water disaster had occurred in Del Rio, which was thirty miles away from us. Suddenly, the water coming out of the tap was brown and full of sediment. I was the closest lab so they contacted me to do the tests. I went and took the samples and began the necessary testing. People began calling me to see if the water was safe to drink.

My mouth fell open as I suddenly realized that I was in a building exactly where I had been in the dream and I was being asked about the safety of the drinking water. I heard my response and knew I had spoken those words in that dream.

"You have to wait for the results. The bacteria need at least a day to grow."

The fact that I had dreamed all of this flooded over me as I realized the implications. If this part of the series could be realized, the rest of the dreams could also be true down to each detail. My concern renewed itself and I watched and wondered carefully at this possibility.

The pink cloud really bothered me. The only pink I have ever seen in real clouds is the pink enveloped in the beautiful sunsets we all love to watch. It made no sense. The clouds in the dream had rolled in with such great force and they had dipped down to the level of the street. I have never seen clouds do that before. What could that possibly be?

Several years later, as I taught a chemistry class, I read something in a chapter that reminded me of something I had forgotten from college. Ionized hydrogen is pink. What ionizes hydrogen? Anything with great amounts of energy ionizes hydrogen.

My mind sought ideas on anything that could produce that much energy. A few possibilities presented themselves to me. Of course, atomic bombs can generate that kind of energy. The world we live in includes ample situations in which an atomic bomb could be sent our way. I thought about what possible targets could be to the west since the cloud had come from the west in the dream. Laughlin Air Force Base is settled approximately thirty miles from Brackettville. That possibility seemed not likely since the Base would not be a strategic strike. However, I am not a military strategist. Who knows what such a strike could do for an enemy?

Another event that could produce such force would be a random meteor strike. Most of us have watched documentaries concerning such catastrophes. Even though we have a few organizations watching for approaching meteors, complete coverage is impossible with the meager resources allotted to these organizations. Often we read about a near miss that nobody even saw coming. There have been fiction stories based on the thought that our government might not see fit to warn us if a meteor was approaching if they could do nothing about it. Certainly, a meteor could strike without warning.

Another scenario which would include a sudden release of massive amounts of energy is the eruption of a super volcano. Yellowstone Park has been revealed to be a super volcano that is due to erupt in its historical cycle. It is also west of Brackettville. This could be another possible source of a pink cloud. Or, a combination of a meteor blast and a super volcano eruption as a result could really belt out the energy.

I still do not even know why I try to figure it out. There is apparently nothing I will be able to do about any of it. I simply know to watch for it and pray. Still, there are parts of the dream series that further confirm their truth.

When Saddam Hussein invaded Kuwait in the early nineties, my husband asked me if that was the man I had seen in my dream. I told him that Saddam was not the man I had seen in the tank. The man I had seen showed a much more determined anger than Saddam ever exhibited. A few years later, I did see the man's face in a documentary...about a young Arab named Bin Laden. At the time, he was nobody newsworthy. I freaked out and started jumping up and down. I ran into the other room where my husband was sitting.

"I know who he is!"
"Who?"
"The man in the tank. His name is Bin Laden."

I am sure that I do not understand all I know about this particular part of my gift. For some reason, I have seen this man since the series of dreams. I never knew what it meant, but I somehow felt a weird sense of connection to him until the time he was killed. When 9/11 occurred and they traced the terrorist attack back to him, it was not a surprise to me. The look on his face in my dream told me that he was quite capable of such activity. And I could tell you that our armed forces would never find Bin Laden in Afghanistan because he was not there. I do not know how I knew this, nor did I know what to do with this information. Nobody wanted to listen.

After Mom's death, I suddenly remembered the dream about a woman on a scooter who would die shortly before the pink cloud arrived. At the time, I knew nobody who was using a scooter, but many years later, as I have already mentioned, my mother became affected with Multiple Sclerosis. At first, she used only a cane but she later required a scooter. I never thought about the dream and the woman on the scooter and put the two together. I am certainly hoping that my fears are not substantiated but I have a nagging feeling that there could soon be a pink cloud in our near future. All I can do is pray and I do that constantly. In a way, the dream comforts me. Yes, I died. But then I stood back up. What a promise!

WHAT I KNOW

Through all of this, there are a few things that I have learned and I have tried to mention some of this as I wrote this story. Still, I would like to reinforce the main ideas surrounding the topic.

First of all, this is a gift from God. I am not responsible for any of the good things He accomplishes through me. I insist that I am not in control and I do not want control. I am quite confident that God has honored my prayer that I would only experience things that He would have me experience, and that I would only use them to His honor and glory. He has protected me from the enemy many times and I know He will continue to do so.

Next, let me address all of the scientists reading this book. I have my degree in Microbiology and am quite aware of the rules of logic and proof in investigation. What I want to stress here is that modern scientists have been consistently making one error in logic. It is completely illogical to assume that something does not exist just because you cannot see it. It is impossible to prove a negative. In order to be good scientists, we must have an open mind.

Think of all the examples of this error in logic. For many centuries, people had no way to "see" air, yet it obviously existed. They had no proof that it was there. The same is true for bacteria and viruses. Did viruses and bacteria not exist simply because we did not have the ability to see them or prove their existence? That is ridiculous, of course. The same error delayed the knowledge of the existence of gorillas for decades. Witnesses reported seeing them but were not believed because, "if they really existed, we would have a skeleton or a body." Today, of course, we all know that gorillas exist. But did they not exist prior to that because we did not have proof? Of course, that is ridiculous.

So, does prophecy exist? Do ghosts exist? Once again, you cannot prove a negative and you must keep an open mind. I have no doubt that someone will find a way to prove all of this someday. In the meantime, you cannot tell me that what I have seen and experienced does not exist. I am sure that goes for everyone who has ever experienced such things.

For those readers who would judge me because they believe that their religion does not have room for modern-day prophecy or ghosts, both are mentioned several times in the Bible. I have heard the argument that prophets only existed in the Old Testament. The Bible clearly tells us that, in the end days, prophets will be increased upon the earth. I know that I am not the only one out there because I personally have found several others.

What about ghosts? Paul describes a conversation he had with a ghost. He writes in 2 Corinthians 12 verse 2 "I knew a man in Christ above fourteen years ago, (whether in the body, I cannot tell, or whether out of the body, I cannot tell: God knoweth;) such a one caught up to the third heaven." Verse 3 continues, "And I knew such a man, (whether in the body or out of the body, I cannot tell: God knoweth;" Verse 4: How that he was caught up in paradise and heard unspeakable words, which it is not lawful for a man to utter." The argument that this man was Christ has a problem because none of the pronouns are capitalized as they usually are when the subject is God or Christ.

I also realize that the Bible instructs us to test the spirits. Let me get this out of the way. Jesus Christ is my Lord. Hopefully that should help some in case someone is thinking that I am being used by the enemy. I am not so worried about what others think of me anymore. I lived my life like that for far too long and now I stand as a witness that God has powers that some would rather not acknowledge. I would rather speak for God than worry about ruffling the feathers of others. It has taken a very long time for me to get to this point, and that I regret. I spent way too much time letting the fears of others stop me from using the gift God has given me.

I can only hope that those with this gift who come after me, including my own children and grandchildren, will gain some strength from listening to my story. I hope they make their stand a little sooner than I did. I believe that the end times are near and that God is going to use each and every one of us in His service during these times.

For those who do not believe, I completely understand and I do not judge you for it. It is easy for me to believe because I actually have experienced these things. I can see that it would be very difficult to believe unless you have seen it firsthand. But do not be surprised when I openly reveal all that I know from experience even though it may make you a little uncomfortable.

I also believe that some who disbelieve the strongest are actually gifted themselves. They argue so strongly against it because they are trying to keep themselves convinced. They simply do not want to face the fact that God may not fit into the manageable little box we want to put Him into. It might mean that He is so magnificent that we cannot control Him. Well, I am here to say, "He is so magnificent that we cannot control Him." He is God and He is omnipotent, whether we understand it or not.

ABOUT THE AUTHOR

Karen Crumley retired after twenty-six years of teaching high school science. She now lives on a ranch in Central Texas where she continues to write. In 2000, she and her husband published a book named Weapon of Jihad http://www.amazon.com/Weapon-Jihad-revised-biowarfare-ebook/dp/B00507U10C/ref=sr_1_1?ie=UTF8&qid=1361296779&sr=8-1&keywords=weapon+of+jihad, which was written as fiction. Later, on 9/11, it proved to be somewhat prophetic.

If you have enjoyed reading this book, please go to Amazon.com and leave a review and a LIKE for me. Also, I would greatly appreciate it if you would tell your friends about it. I am presently collecting material for a sequel to this book as the weirdness continues daily and I continue to document it. If you would like to leave a message for me, you may do so on my blog, http://growingupweirdmedium.wordpress.com/ or on my Facebook author page, https://www.facebook.com/pages/Karen-Crumley-author/261297727233316?ref=hl

www.ingramcontent.com/pod-product-compliance
Lightning Source LLC
Chambersburg PA
CBHW061645040426
42446CB00010B/1589